The Oldest City's Oldest Synagogue

Robert Blau

Published by Robert Blau, 2023.

THE OLDEST CITY'S OLDEST SYNAGOGUE

First edition. October 31, 2023.

ISBN: 979-8223735717

Written by Robert Blau.

Table of Contents

To all former and current members of First Congregation Sons of Israel

<u>The Oldest City's Oldest Synagogue</u>

By Robert Blau

FOREWARD

The idea for this book came about at a meeting in early July, 2023, to discuss the leadership change at First Congregation Sons of Israel that would be underway a few months later. Longtime synagogue president, Les Stern, and longtime treasurer, Karen Stern, would not only be stepping down from their official positions, but also moving halfway across the country. Concerned members of the congregation, led by Les' eventual successor, Barry Broudy, discussed a full list of tasks, up until then performed by Les and Karen, that would have to be distributed among a new set of officials, most of whom would need to make themselves candidates in the August membership elections.

Understand that these elections are not so much a function of competing individuals or factions, but rather of who wants to put their name on the ballot, unopposed, to sign up for tons of uncompensated volunteer work, motivated mostly by dedication to the synagogue, and maybe a small amount of masochism.

Besides agreeing myself to run for one of the open trustee positions, I spoke up at the meeting to ask Les if his encyclopedic knowledge of the synagogue's history was based on any written reference works or was mostly in his head. I mentioned how impressed I was by his discourse the previous Sabbath morning service about the history of the sanctuary's beautiful stained-glass windows (see chapter 5). When Les answered that it was largely information in his head, I proposed to write a book on the synagogue's history, with my research to begin by picking Les' brains in a sit-down interview before he left town. This elicited an enthusiastic response from all those present at the meeting, some of whom had excellent ideas as to places where I could find primary sources and other documented information. The University of Florida has a Judaica library, for example. Also, current congregants that are descendants of the founding families would be willing and eager to talk to me and get their oral histories incorporated into the narrative.

At that point I was committed to the project, which as it turns out, coincides with the 100th anniversary of the opening of First Congregation Sons of Israel on Cordova Street in downtown St. Augustine. It is, of course, impressive that the synagogue we attend is a 100-year old building; but that could easily be lost in the shuffle of *much older* structures and landmarks in St. Augustine, which was founded by Spanish settlers in 1565. Hopefully, this book will draw favorable attention to this very special part of "America's Oldest City's" history, and ideally contribute to First Congregation Sons of Israel living to celebrate another hundred years in 2124.

Barry Broudy Presenting Recognition Award

To Karen and Les Stern, August 20, 2023 [1]

Saint Augustine

October 2023

1. INTRODUCTION

Saint Augustine, Florida is a city steeped in history. Its main industry, tourism, is based on the city's origins in 1565, making it the oldest continuously inhabited European (and African) settlement in the continental United States. Visitors come from all over the country and all over the world to visit the Spanish colonial sector, which includes the oldest street, house, and schoolhouse in the country. Over 800,000 tourists per year visit Castillo San Marcos, the Spanish fort, the first phase of which was built from 1672 to 1695. That is almost three times the population of St. Johns County, where Saint Augustine sits. Nowadays the Castillo is administered by the National Park Service; since its inception it has been held by Spain, England, Spain again, and then sold to the United States as part of the 1819 Adams-Onís Treaty, which got us all of Florida (from Spain) for five million dollars. Adams was future President John Quincy Adams, who at the time was Secretary of State in the Monroe Administration; Luís de Onís was the Spanish Ambassador with authority to sign for the Kingdom of Spain. The time period is referred to by historians as "The Era of Good Feeling."

The King and Queen of Spain Visit Castillo San

Marcos in 2015, on St. Augustine's 450th anniversary

(Photo by author from Castillo San Marcos Volunteer Room display)

In that context, the first religious service at First Congregation Sons of Israel, in March of 1924, seems like a relatively recent phenomenon. Even so, its founding is a fascinating story, and the building itself is a beautiful structure, especially its stained-glass windows, which as you will see, have a story all their own. Visitors to Saint Augustine will often include a stop at the synagogue, on Cordova Street in the downtown area, as part of their overall immersion into The Oldest City's history. The script for those tours could serve as a "Cliff Notes" version of this book, while the beginning of the tour, in what has been the rabbi's study, includes some photos of the original, founding families from the Jewish community.

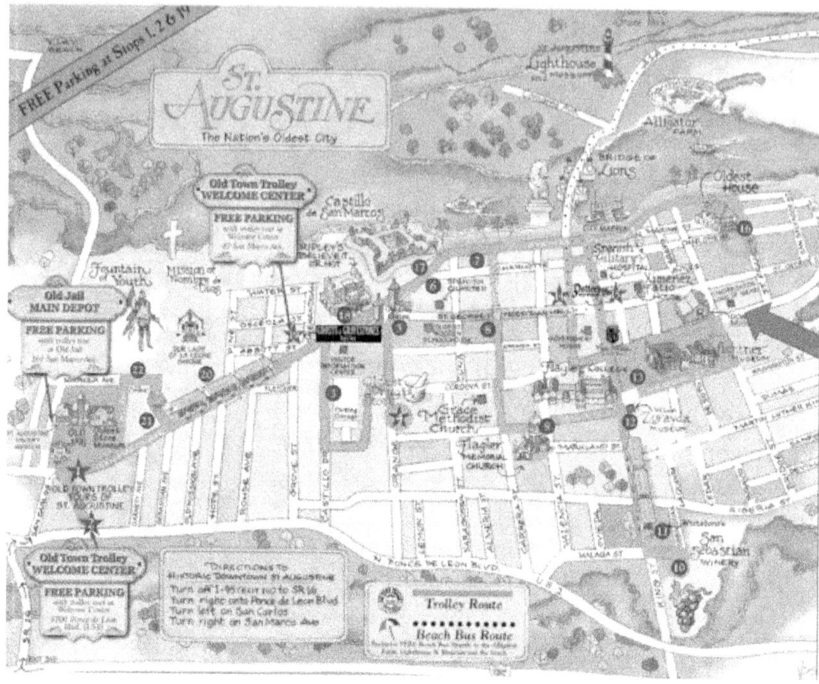

The blue arrow points to the synagogue's location on the St. Augustine Tourist Map [2]

2. ORIGINS

There is some evidence that indicates a Jewish presence among the early Spanish settlers in Saint Augustine. The Saint Augustine Jewish Historical Society has compiled some documentation on this subject.[3] The settlers in question would have been "crypto" Jews, (Marranos or Conversos) who were of Jewish ancestry but by the 16th century were practicing Catholics. Their families' conversion to Christianity was to protect them from the cruelties visited upon Jews during the Spanish Inquisition. It didn't always succeed, and Marranos, as well as practicing Jews, were imprisoned, executed, or expelled from Spain during that time. In the mid- to late-18th century, settlers from the Spanish Island of Minorca were given land in Eastern Florida, and a census from the year 1813 indicates that some of these, based on their surnames, may have had Jewish blood.[4] The Spanish Inquisition has been lampooned by the Monty Python comedy troupe ("Nobody expects the Spanish Inquisition") and by Mel Brooks in his movie "History of the World." Nowadays we can laugh at this kind of gallows humor, but at the time it really was a matter of life and death for Jews. If some of them made a half-hearted conversion, and eventually they or their descendants made it to Saint Augustine, then they should be celebrated for their will to survive.

The early to mid-19th century brought two of the most well-known Jews to Northeast Florida: Moises Elias Levy, originally from Morocco, via the Caribbean (where he was a big success in the timber industry); and his son David Levy Yulee, who became Florida's first U.S. Senator, and also the first Jewish U.S. Senator. They lived a part of their lives in St. Augustine, but did not live to see a permanent Jewish community take root there.[5]

The Jewish émigrés who became the founders of Saint Augustine's modern Jewish community were largely from Eastern Europe, and came to the New World in the latter part of the 19th Century. This was a time and a place in Jewish history just as bad as the Inquisition. Jews in Russia and nearby areas known as the "Pale of Settlement" were treated as second-class citizens, and were the object of violent riots called "pogroms," leaving death and destruction in their wake. The Broadway musical (and film adaptation) "Fiddler on the Roof" depicts the poverty and terrorizing of a small Jewish town in Russia by agents of or allied with the Czar of Russia. At a poignant moment in the story a villager asks their rabbi if there is a prayer for the Czar, to which the rabbi replies: "May the Lord bless and keep the Czar...far away from us."

THE PALE 1835–1917
0 200
Miles
St. Petersburg
1891 2,000 Jews deported, many of them in chains
1865 Open to Jews
Moscow
1891 20,000 Jews expelled
Baltic Sea
GERMANY
KOVNO
VITEBSK
SUWALKI
VILNA
MOGILEV
PLOCK
LOMZA
WARSAW
GRODNO
MINSK
KALISZ
SYEDLITZ
PIOTRKOW
RADOM
KIELCE
LUBLIN
CHERNIGOV
VOLHYNIA
Brody
Kiev
POLTAVA
AUSTRIA-HUNGARY
KIEV
PODOLIA
EKATERINOSLAV
BESSARABIA
KHERSON
Nikolaev
RUMANIA
TAURIDA
Sebastopol
Yalta
Black Sea
Principal town from which in 1880 began the exodus of over two million Jews from the Pale to the United States, Britain, Europe, South America, and Palestine
In 1882 500,000 Jews living in rural areas of the Pale were forced to leave their homes and live in towns or townlets (shtetls) in the Pale. 250,000 Jews living along the western frontier of Russia were also moved into the Pale. 700,000 Jews living east of the Pale were driven into the Pale by 1891
The Pale of Settlement. Russian Jews confined to this area by laws of 1795 and 1835. By 1885 there were over 4 million Jews living in the Pale
Towns within the Pale barred to Jews without special residence permits

This map, and associated captions, taken from the online "Jewish Virtual Library,"[6] shows the region of Eastern Europe, including Russia, where Jews were both ghetto-ized and expelled. Consistent with the inset captions, over two million Jews from this area emigrated to the United States between 1880 and 1914. This was the enormous wave of Jewish immigrants that included the group that made its way to Northeast Florida.

(...continuing our narrative...)

Well, as it turned out, St. Augustine, Florida was far enough away from the Czar to become a relatively safe, new home for dozens of Jewish families, among them the founding families of what would later become First Congregation Sons of Israel. Besides fleeing persecution, they also came to America, like so many immigrants before and after them, to find economic opportunity. And, like Jews in other places in the United States, they became small businessmen and professionals, and also did their best to keep their religious faith and practices alive in an environment where almost all of their neighbors were Catholics. Until the actual building of a synagogue, keeping the faith alive was a matter of meeting in each other's homes, using Torah scrolls[7] that they had brought with them when they crossed the Atlantic. Those very same Torah scrolls are the ones still in use currently at First Congregations Sons of Israel.

At about this same time in St. Augustine's history, legendary Florida developer Henry Flagler was putting the city on the map as a prime tourist location for Americans from the Northeast, principally New York City. His mega-investments in railroads and hotels created a golden age for this part of Florida, with the two main attractions being the ornate, Spanish-style Ponce de Leon and Alcazar hotels in downtown St. Augustine. These were state-of-the art structures, with the most modern furnishings, lighting and plumbing fixtures, to ensure the comfort of the high-society guests. The Alcazar Hotel had the world's largest indoor swimming pool, which is today a restaurant on the lower level of what is now the Lightner Museum. The Ponce de Leon Hotel closed in 1967, and its buildings became part of Flagler College. Both are walking distance from First Congregation Sons of Israel, with the east side of the museum sharing a block of Cordova Street just north of the synagogue.

The Lightner Museum, formerly the Alcazar Hotel [8]

To the extent that the St. Augustine Jewish community has a George Washington-esque figure, that would be Jacob Tarlinsky. Tarlinsky was the unquestioned leader of the community, and the one who brought the Torah scrolls to St. Augustine. His house would be the most common place for religious services before a synagogue would eventually be built.

Rosh Hoshannah Begins at Sundown Today

At sundown this evening the Jewish new year, 5,670, will be ushered in and will be observed here by the orthodox Hebrews. All of the Jewish merchants who conform to the Hebrew faith will close their places of business. Services will be held at the home of Jacob Tarlinsky on Washington street.

This opens the Hebrew holiday season, which lasts on through the Penitential Days, ending with the observance of Yom Kipper, or the Day of Atonement on Sept. 25.

The Feast of Rosh Hoshannah begins this evening at 6 o'clock and continues through Thursday and Friday, which are the 2d and 3d of the month Tishri of the Jewish calendar. The ritual for the New Year's service, the authorship of which is covered in a mist of tradition, is the most beautiful in the Jewish prayer book.

The sounding of the ram's horn in commemoration of the Biblical incident in which Abraham started to offer up his son Isaac in accordance with the Divine wish, but was allowed instead to offer a lamb, is one of the impressive features of this service.

The two days of the Feast of Rosh Hoshannah, Thursday and Friday, are days given up to reflection. Through these days and the Penitential period which does not end until Yom Kippur, there is a special feature of the services each day, both in the morning and in the evening.

Rosh Hoshannah usually ends on the third day of the month Tishri, Sept. 18, with the Fast of Guedaliah. Because the date falls on the Jewish Sabbath this year, however, the following day will be observed instead. The fast begins Saturday evening at sundown and lasts through Sunday and is strictly observed.

The Penitential Days end on the tenth day of Tishri, which is the 25th of September. That is Yom Kippur, the Day of Atonement. The entire period observed with special prayers of supplication at the two daily services.

The Jewish colony here is steadily increasing and their numbers now justify the proper observanse of the Hebrew feast periods.

1909 Jewish New Year Observed at Tarlinsky Home [9]

Jacob Tarlinsky was born in 1861 in Olinka, which was in a region of modern-day Poland that was part of the Russian empire at the time. He emigrated to the United States in 1886, during the first Grover Cleveland Administration, living initially in Brooklyn, NY before moving south to Florida. Tarlinsky opened a bargain store on the corner of Bridge and Washington Streets in 1905. In a University of North Florida research paper regarding Black-owned businesses in the historic Lincolnville neighborhood in St. Augustine, Tarlinsky is mentioned as running a successful discount store, but also making a favorable impression with his customers, black and white alike.[10] His wife, Dora (born in Russia in 1862), was also a powerful force in establishing businesses in St. Augustine, particularly selecting properties for both residential and commercial use. She purchased the famous Lorillard Villa on St. George Street, for example, and raised her family there. Dora's strong business acumen would be passed on to the three Tarlinsky daughters: Lena, Florence, and Sara. Jacob would live until 1927, leaving behind the great legacy of having organized the St. Augustine Jewish community into an incorporated entity, to be followed by the acquisition of a burial ground and a synagogue structure. Read on to find out more about the Tarlinsky family through the generations.

Dora and Jacob Tarlinsky [11]

A vivid description of life among the early Jewish settlers is recorded in a transcript of an oral interview of Mary Safer in 1989. The interviewer was Samuel Proctor, who founded the Oral History Program at the University of Florida that bears his name. Proctor himself grew up in St. Augustine and was part of the Jewish community that he was researching.

Mary Safer was born in Newark, NJ in 1904, and came to Saint Augustine in 1907. Her parents were Esther and Morris Friedman, who immigrated to the United States from Hungary in 1888. The family already had a presence in Saint Augustine; Ida and David Gerstel, Mary's aunt and uncle, owned and managed the Lynn Hotel on St. George Street. Other Jewish families already there besides the Tarlinskys were the Lews, Effs, Pinkosons and Mehlmans.

Mary Safer's family originally was in the fruit business, but then opened a cleaning, pressing and tailoring store on Aviles Street (identified on all the tourist maps as the nation's oldest street). As was the custom at that time, the family's residence was right over the store. Additionally, Mary's parents operated the Chautauqua Hotel on King Street, near what is currently Constitution Plaza in the heart of downtown. It cost 50 cents a night to stay there; Samuel Proctor noted that his parents stayed there during their honeymoon. One of the hotel's most storied guests was Minnie Marx, Groucho's mother.

Minnie Marx + Groucho Marx [12]

Bonus Groucho quote: "Outside of a dog, a book is a man's best friend; inside of a dog, it's too dark to read."

Mary remembers herself and her disabled brother, on account of their Jewish identities, being the object of ridicule and bullying by a nasty group of Catholic schoolboys. It left a painful memory from what was otherwise a normal, healthy childhood. On the positive side, as an adolescent in love with history, Mary remembers serving as a tour guide at Castillo San Marcos for guests at the Chautauqua Hotel. She also remembers her father, Morris Friedman, becoming president of the congregation, and spending an inordinate amount of time taking care of cemetery and synagogue affairs, after both were formally up and running.

The St. Augustine Jewish families, besides their closeness with each other, kept kosher and followed Jewish traditions, for example, closing businesses on important holidays. For religious services they would walk to the makeshift synagogue at the Tarlinsky's home/business (which had been hosting religious services as early as 1898), even after some of them were wealthy enough to own a car. It wasn't too much of a hardship, as they all lived within walking distance of each other, which today would still be walking distance to the synagogue on Cordova Street. The original kosher butcher was Morris Jaffe, father of long-time synagogue patron and leader, Max Jaffe. Until the first rabbi came to the two-year-old synagogue in 1926, the kosher butcher would carry out some rabbinical functions. For weddings and Bar Mitzvahs they would bring in a rabbi from Jacksonville.[13]

On December 14, 1908, Mr. Tarlinsky filed an article of incorporation with St. Johns County to create and formalize the Jewish community.

His name, as well as the names of co-signers and the first set of officers, are shown in this official document:

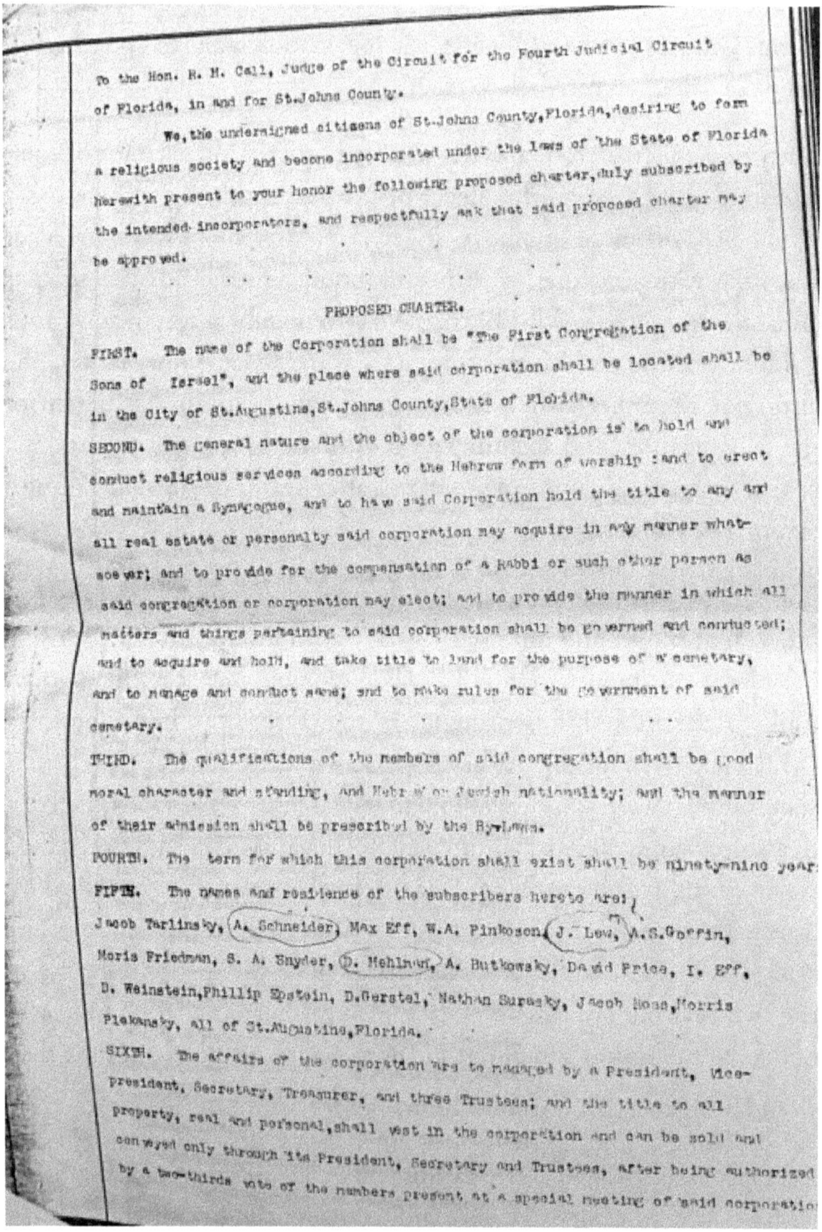

To the Hon. R. M. Call, Judge of the Circuit for the Fourth Judicial Circuit of Florida, in and for St.Johns County.

We, the undersigned citizens of St.Johns County, Florida, desiring to form a religious society and become incorporated under the laws of the State of Florida herewith present to your honor the following proposed charter, duly subscribed by the intended incorporators, and respectfully ask that said proposed charter may be approved.

PROPOSED CHARTER.

FIRST. The name of the Corporation shall be "The First Congregation of the Sons of Israel", and the place where said corporation shall be located shall be in the City of St.Augustine, St.Johns County, State of Florida.

SECOND. The general nature and the object of the corporation is to hold and conduct religious services according to the Hebrew form of worship; and to erect and maintain a Synagogue, and to have said Corporation hold the title to any and all real estate or personalty said corporation may acquire in any manner whatsoever; and to provide for the compensation of a Rabbi or such other person as said congregation or corporation may elect; and to provide the manner in which all matters and things pertaining to said corporation shall be governed and conducted; and to acquire and hold, and take title to land for the purpose of a cemetary, and to manage and conduct same; and to make rules for the government of said cemetary.

THIRD. The qualifications of the members of said congregation shall be good moral character and standing, and Hebrew or Jewish nationality; and the manner of their admission shall be prescribed by the By-Laws.

FOURTH. The term for which this corporation shall exist shall be ninety-nine year[illegible]

FIFTH. The names and residence of the subscribers hereto are:

Jacob Tarlinsky, A. Schneider, Max Eff, W.A. Pinkoson, J. Lew, A.S.Goffin, Moris Friedman, S. A. Snyder, D. Mehlman, A. Butkowsky, David Price, I. Eff, D. Weinstein, Phillip Epstein, D.Gerstel, Nathan Suresky, Jacob Ross, Morris Plekansky, all of St.Augustine, Florida.

SIXTH. The affairs of the corporation are to managed by a President, Vice-president, Secretary, Treasurer, and three Trustees; and the title to all property, real and personal, shall vest in the corporation and can be sold and conveyed only through its President, Secretary and Trustees, after being authorized by a two-thirds vote of the members present at a special meeting of said corporatio[illegible] called for that purpose. And all of said officers shall be elected by the congregation and the First Sunday in April and October of each and every year unless otherwise provided by the By-Laws.

SEVENTH. THE officers who are to manage the affairs of said corporation and the Trustees thereof, until the first election under the charter, shall be:

Jacob Tarlinsky, President, A. Schneider, Vice President, Max Eff, Treasurer, W. A. Pinkoson, Secretary, and J. Lew, A.S.Goffin, Morris Friedman, Trustees.

EIGHTH. The By-Laws of the corporation are to be altered or recinded by a majority of the congregation at a meeting thereof called for such purposes.

NINTH. The highest amount of indebtedness or liability to which the corporation can at any time subject itself shall not be greater than two thirds of the value of the property held by said corporation.

TENTH. The amount in value of real estate which said corporation may hold shall be twenty thousand dollars, subject always to the approval of the Circuit Judge of the Fourth Judicial District of Florida.

Jacob Tarlinsky ------ of St.Augustine, Florida.
A. Schneider ---------- of St.Augustine, Florida.
Max Eff---------------- of St.Augustine, Florida.
W.A.Pinkoson----------- of St.Augustine, Florida.
J. A. Lew-------------- of St.Augustine, Florida.
A.S.Goffin------------- of St.Augustine, Florida.
Morris Friedman-------- of St.Augustine, Florida.
S.A.Snyder ------------ of St.Augustine, Florida.
D. Mehlman------------- of St.Augustine, Florida.
A. Butkowsky----------- of St.Augustine, Florida.
Philip Epstein--------- of St.Augustine, Florida.
David Price------------ of St.Augustine, Florida.
I.Eff------------------ of St.Augustine, Florida.
D.Weinstein------------ of St.Augustine, Florida.
Nathan Surasky--------- of St.Augustine, Florida.
Morris Piskansky ------ of St.Augustine, Florida.
David Gerstel --------- of St.Augustine, Florida.
J. Ross --------------- of St.Augustine, Florida.

STATE OF FLORIDA
:
ST. JOHNS COUNTY.

On this day personally appeared before me, W. A. MacWilliam, a Notary Public in and for said State at large, Jacob Tarlinsky, who being by me first duly sworn, deposes and says, that he is one of the subscribers to the proposed charter, and that it is intended in good faith to carry out the purposes and objects set forth therein.

Jacob Tarlinsky.

Sworn to and subscribed before me this 14th day of December, A.D., 1908.

W. A. MacWilliams
Notary Public State of Florida at Large.

Approved
R. M. Call,
Judge.

(official seal)

Jan. 18th. 1908.

Filed Dec. 15th. 1908.

A True Record.

H. Wallace Shaw
CLERK CIRCUIT COURT.

[14]

3. CEMETERY

Before any money would be raised or work be done to build a synagogue building, the community's first order of significant business was to obtain a burial ground. The cemetery land in question had been considered consecrated ground even before it became the property of the Saint Augustine Jewish community. A Jewish peddler, Gershom Posenansky, who was killed during the Second Seminole Indian War, was buried there in 1840. There is some information that points to the possibility that three Jewish Confederate soldiers were buried there as well. The land was originally owned by the railroad company, then it passed to a family from Wisconsin, who in turn, sold it to the recently established Jewish congregation sometime in early 1911. The first official burial there of an FCSI member was in March, 1911. The deceased was Abe Schneider (Mary Safer's great uncle), a deputy sheriff who was killed during a train robbery in nearby Espanola[15]. The cemetery's masonry retaining wall was built in 1919.

Much of the history of First Congregation Sons of Israel can be learned just by taking a stroll through the cemetery, as the grave markers of the founding members are all there, with information about their date and place of birth, and of course the date they passed away. The cemetery's location is on Evergreen Avenue in the West King St. area of St. Augustine. The many shade trees provide a pretty, tranquil setting. A photo of the entrance-way is shown below.

Cemetery Entrance Gate on Evergreen Avenue[16]

In 1946, the FCSI congregation officially created the "Sons of Israel Cemetery Association," as indicated by this 1957 memorandum shown below, in which the Cemetery Association is reconstituted.

Subject: "Sons of Israel Cemetery Association"

History: On December 13, 1840, a young single man, probably a peddler, was murdered in ambush by Indians on the highway in the vicinity of St. Augustine, Florida.

These were the facts gathered by the handful of Jews of St. Augustine from a lone tombstone, broken in several pieces, early in the 20th century. They put the pieces together, read the inscription and had a replica made. These Jewish citizens proceeded to obtain a tract of land from St. Johns County which surrounded this grave; and it became what is now the Cemetery of The First Congregation of the Sons of Israel. The next burial occurred in 1911. Today, April 5, 1957, there are just over seventy graves in the Cemetery.

Over the years, several half-hearted attempts have been initiated to improve and beautify the Cemetery property. The net results, while substantial, are only a beginning. One section of the land has been fenced. City water has been piped in. The fenced-in section has been subdivided into lots and blocks with an ornamental center and embellished with shrubbery. Clearly defined paths run through this section. The grass has been kept cut and weeds have been kept down.

On November 17, 1946, as authorized by motion of the Congregation, a meeting was held with its purpose to organize the "Sons of Israel Cemetery Association." Invited to this meeting were all members of the Jewish community, either with personal or esthetic interest in the Cemetery. Unanimously, it was voted to form the association.

By motion, duly carried, it was voted to set membership dues at $10 a year; and a committee was appointed to contact out-of-town prospective members.

The purposes of the association, as set forth, were as follows:

1. To maintain perpetual upkeep of the Cemetery property,
   a. by keeping grass planted, watered and cut throughout the year,
   b. by keeping gate and fence in good repair
   c. by proper landscaping
2. To limit care of individual graves and plots to Association Members.

In that year approximately twenty persons indicated willingness to support the association and paid their dues. $285 was raised that year--barely enough to plant some winter rye grass and to keep it cut. After December 29, 1947, the association was allowed to lapse and little money was collected for upkeep purposes.

→ On March 7, 1957, the Congregation, at a regular meeting, again voted unanimously to permit the formation of a "Cemetery Association", possibly in the form of a corporation, subsidiary to it, and to which the Congregation would grant control of the Cemetery property for the purpose of providing for its maintenance in annual and perpetual upkeep, to make rules for its operation and to set up a schedule of prices for graves and plots and reserving for Congregation Members right to free burial "in sequence" with the stipulation that the right to reserve a particular grave is limited only to the surviving widow, widower and children under eighteen.

→ Two facts contributed to the new impetus to implement the formation of the association:

1. The A. S. Weinstein family purchased land for $1000, and the money was placed in a Trust Fund for Perpetual Upkeep.
2. Charles Goldfine, of Philadelphia, made a gift of $250 to the Trust Fund.

You are now up-to-date on what has transpired in reference "Formation of Cemetery Association." [17]

Nowadays, there is a subset of the overall FSCI governing board that has responsibility for the cemetery. This includes responding to requests for burials, usually, but not always, of members of the congregation. This has to be done promptly, as Jewish tradition (sometimes honored in the breach), calls for burial with 24 hours of death. The cemetery also requires upkeep, which in 2022 necessitated a major repair of the retaining wall on the south side of the burial ground, as Hurricane Ian caused a large tree to fall in that area.

Parallel to the cemetery is a memorial plaque board in the rear of the sanctuary, replete with names of deceased congregants and their relatives. To commission a new plaque, a surviving relative makes a donation to the synagogue, and then the information about the deceased is sent to a local engraving company. The board was modernized in 2019, in such a way that a light will glow next to any name on the board during the week of that person's death anniversary ("Yahrtzeit").

Memorial boards reinstalled at First Congregation Sons of Israel in St. Augustine

By Sons of Israel

First Congregation Sons of Israel in St. Augustine is working on the reinstallation and programming of the Yartzeit memorial boards in the newly restored sanctuary. The boards were taken down after losing electricity and having water damage from Hurricane Matthew in October 2016. The light bars were sent to W&E Baum in New Jersey for clean-up and programming before being reinstalled.

Maurice Zagha, a principal of W&E Baum, made a special trip from New Jersey to help install, connect and program the boards with the help of congregation members Les Stern, Reggie Daniels and Frank Wiener. The name plates will be put up with help from congregation member volunteers.

First Congregation Sons of Israel is located at 161 Cordova Street in historic St. Augustine. For more information visit www.firstcongregation-sonsofisrael.com or call 904-829-9552.

News Report/Photo of Memorial Board Upgrade[18]

Simone Broudy-Kilbourn (with an assist from Howard Strickland) has done extensive research regarding the cemetery, and compiled a map of all the gravesites, as of 2008. The images below show the cemetery divided into four quadrants: Southeast; Northeast; Southwest; and Northwest. You can find the two original gravesites—Posenansky and Schneider—in the lower right-hand corner of the Southwest quadrant.

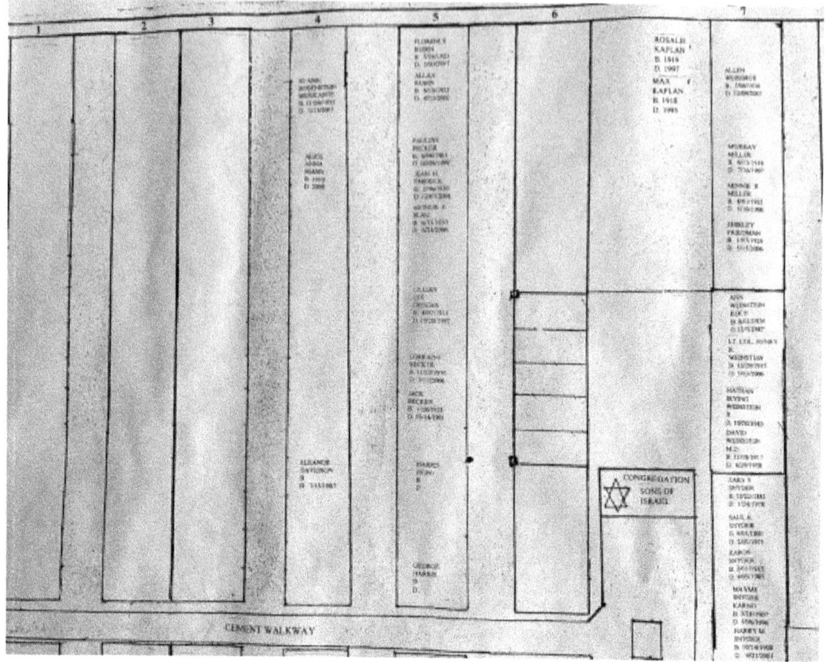

Cemetery Southeast

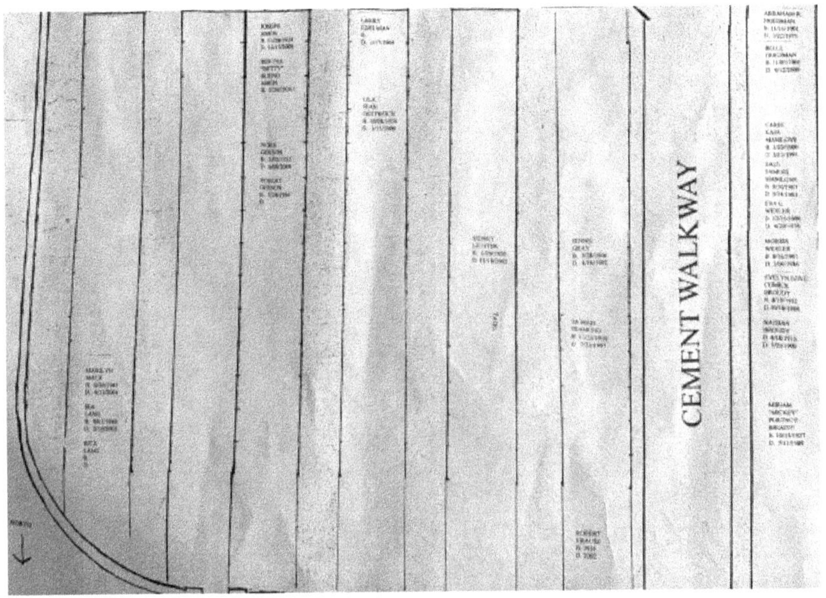

Cemetery Northeast

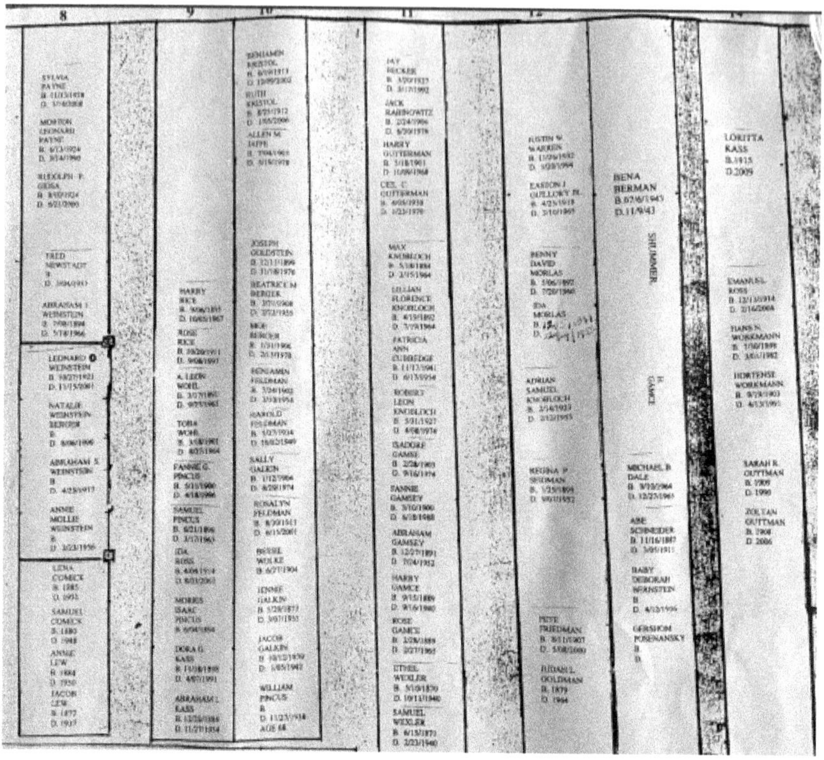

8

SYLVIA PAYNE

MORTON LEONARD PAYNE

RUDOLPH F. GIDSA

FRED NEWSTADT

ABRAHAM I. WEINSTEIN

LEONARD WEINSTEIN

NATALIE WEINSTEIN-BERGER

ABRAHAM S. WEINSTEIN

ANNIE MOLLIE WEINSTEIN

LENA COMICK

SAMUEL COMICK

ANNIE LEW

JACOB LEW

9

HARRY RICE

ROSE RICE

A. LEON WOHL

TOBA WOHL

FANNIE G. PINCUS

SAMUEL PINCUS

IDA ROSS

MORRIS ISAAC PINCUS

DORA G. KASS

ABRAHAM I. KASS

10

BENJAMIN KRISTOL

RUTH KRISTOL

ALLEN M. JAFFE

JOSEPH GOLDSTEIN

BEATRICE M. BERGER

MAX BERGER

BENJAMIN FELDMAN

HAROLD FELDMAN

SALLY GALKIN

ROSALYN FELDMAN

BESSIE WOLKE

JENNIE GALKIN

JACOB GALKIN

WILLIAM PINCUS
D. 11/23/1918
AGE 68

11

JAY BECKER

JACK RABINOWITZ

HARRY GUTTERMAN

CEIL C. GUTTERMAN

MAX KNOBLOCH

LILLIAN FLORENCE KNOBLOCH

PATRICIA ANN CURREDGE

ROBERT LEON KNOBLOCH

ISADORE GAMSE

FANNIE GAMSEY

ABRAHAM GAMSEY

HARRY GAMCE

ROSE GAMCE

ETHEL WEXLER

SAMUEL WEXLER

12

JUSTIN W. WARREN

EASTON J. GUILLORY JR.

BENNY DAVID MORLAS

IDA MORLAS

ADRIAN SAMUEL KNOBLOCH

REGINA P. SEIDMAN

PETE FRIEDMAN

JUDAH L. GOLDMAN
B. 1879
D. 1944

BENA BERMAN
B.07/6/1943
D.11/9/43

SHLIMMER

H. GAMCE

MICHAEL B. DALE

ABE SCHNEIDER

BABY DEBORAH WEINSTEIN

GERSHOM POSENANSKY

14

LORITTA KASS
B.1915
D.2009

EMANUEL ROSS

HANS N. WORKMANN

HORTENSE WORKMANN

SARAH R. GUTTMAN
B. 1909
D. 1990

ZOLTAN GUTTMAN
B. 1908
D. 2006

Cemetery Southwest

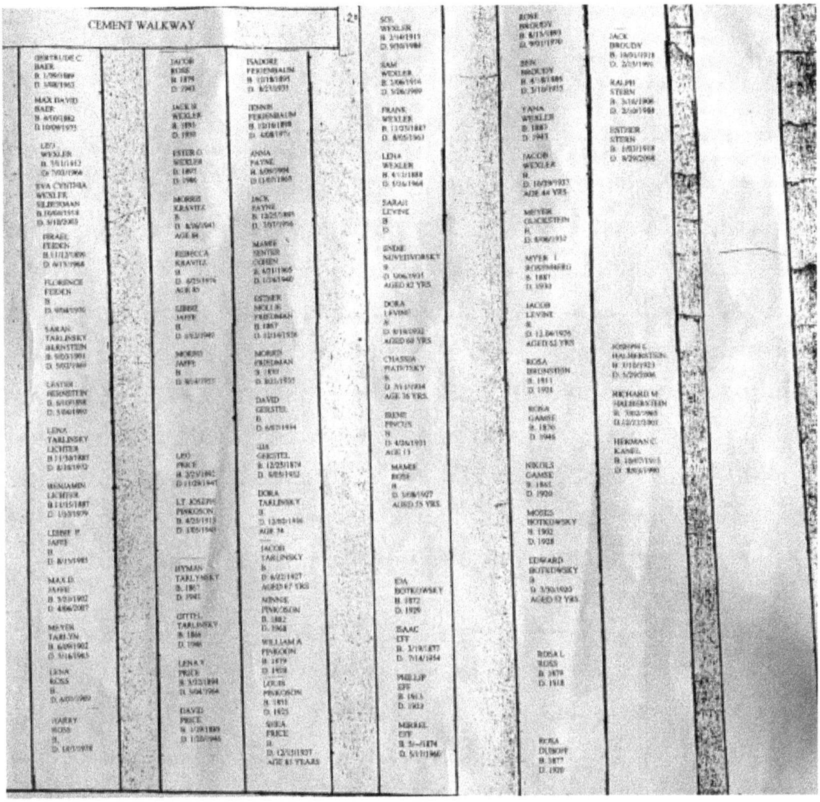

Cemetery Northwest [19]

4. SYNAGOGUE BUILDING

In 1919 the community purchased the site (Morris Jaffe's property) for the permanent synagogue building, and raised 14,000 dollars for that project. On March 24, 1923, they hired Jim Keller as the contractor and Francis A. Hollingsworth as the architect. Hollingsworth was one of the most well-known and experienced architects in Saint Augustine. During his lifetime (1885-1974) he designed many other well-known buildings in the area: The State Arsenal Building; Mark W. Lance Armory; Ketterlinus High School; First National Bank; Peoples Bank; The St. Augustine Record Building; The Pier and Recreation Center at St. Augustine Beach; R.B Hunt Elementary School; St. Augustine High School; and other structures in Palatka and Hastings.

The cornerstone for the synagogue was laid on May 3, 1923, at a ceremony led by FCSI's own Jacob A. Lew, with the presence of Rabbi C. A. Press, of Congregation B'nai Israel in Jacksonville, and St. Augustine Mayor Peter Perry. The most iconic photo from that era (shown below) records the synagogue's dedication ceremony, in October, 1923, in which the entire original membership was present. An article in the St. Augustine Evening Record of January 17, 1924 reports the near completion of the synagogue, at a cost of between 12,000 and 13,000 dollars; with a follow-up on its completion on January 31, 1924. The first service would be held two months later, on March 30, 1924.[20] Because of both the religious prohibition against driving cars on the Sabbath and the fact that all the charter-member families lived close by, the builders and architect left very little space for parking. Fast forward to the 21st Century and that still is not much of a problem most of the year. On Rosh Hashana and Yom Kippur, however, when the full membership tends to show up, there is not nearly enough parking space.

The address is 161 Cordova Street, which it fitting, as Córdoba[21], Spain was a center of Jewish culture and learning in the middle ages. Moises Maimonides, one of Jewry's greatest Talmudic scholars, was born and raised in Córdoba. Here is a photo of a statue of Maimonides in modern-day Córdoba:

[22]

The FCSI building's structure would conform to the layout of an Orthodox synagogue, which was the life- and worship style of the founding members. This meant that a second, balcony level, was built for women and children, who would be separated from their husbands and fathers during religious services. The pulpit was in the middle of the lower level, with seats (purchased from a local movie theater) radiating out from there. Also, on the lower level was a ritual bath for women ("Mikveh"), which later was bricked over during a renovation in the 1950s.

After World War II, the congregation decided to reorient itself as Conservative, first with a half-way measure that allowed women to sit on the main level of the sanctuary, but on one side, separated from the men on the other side by a divider and opaque screen that ran down the center aisle. Currently, FCSI is identified as Conservative-Egalitarian, which means that women and men can sit together during services, and women can also: 1) be counted among the ten-minimum to form a "minyan" (minion, but not to be confused with the cartoon minion characters), or quorum to be able to hold an unabridged service; and 2) be called up to read from the Torah and even preside over religious services. One of the two regular visiting rabbis currently is a woman, Rabbi Mona Decker from Jacksonville. With the change from Orthodox to Conservative, the interior of the synagogue was redesigned to place the pulpit in the front (the East end of the sanctuary) and have the seats lined up in rows facing the front.

First Congregation Sons of Israel Today - Exterior [23]

FCSI Today – Interior [24]

Winston Churchill once wrote, famously, that if there were a country of three Jews, then they would be President, Vice-President, and Leader of the Opposition party. And so it is that Orthodox, Conservative, and Reform are a continuum of Jewish worship and lifestyle that in some places serve as unbridgeable fault lines among 21st Century Jews. In brief, Orthodox are the most strictly observant, with services almost entirely in Hebrew, and rules about what can and cannot be done on the Sabbath dutifully followed. They follow kosher laws to the letter, tend to marry among themselves and have many children. Reform Judaism is the opposite extreme, using much more English than Hebrew in worship, not following kosher dietary rules, frequently intermarrying, etc. Conservatives are somewhere in the middle. Although, as noted above, FCSI migrated from Orthodox to Conservative in the 1940s, it wasn't until 2012 that the congregation affiliated formally with the "United Synagogues of Conservative Judaism."

Affiliation Certificate from 2012 [25]

Interestingly, there is a correlation between Jewish religious orthodoxy and political affiliation in the United States. Orthodox tend to vote Republican; Reformed for Democrats; Conservatives are the swing votes. Very importantly, it is FCSI policy to keep politics out of the sanctuary. Consistent with Conservative Jewish strictures, rabbis at

FCSI do not perform mixed-marriage weddings; and only bona-fide Jews can be buried at the St. Augustine Jewish cemetery.

Another fault line among Jews is between Ashkenazi and Sephardic. Very briefly, the former are from Central and Eastern Europe; the latter from Spain (the word "Sepharad" means Spain in Hebrew), North Africa and the Middle East.[26] Ashkenazi Jews are the ones who spoke/speak Yiddish, a lingua franca that combines Hebrew with European languages, mostly German. Words like bagel, chutzpah, mensch, nosh, schlemiel and schmooze come from Yiddish[27]. Hebrew itself has Ashkenazi and Sephardic pronunciations, with the latter becoming the more common usage over time in American synagogues. To an Ashkenazi, the Sabbath is "Shabbos;" to a Sephardic it is "Shabbat," for example. The founding families of First Congregations Sons of Israel were all Ashkenazi; however, over time, the congregation has become more diverse. The rabbis who preside over FCSI religious services nowadays use Sephardic Hebrew pronunciation.

For much of its history, FCSI was the only synagogue in Saint Augustine. That changed in 1993, with the founding of a Reform congregation, Bet Yam ("House by the Sea"). Then, in 2014, the Orthodox-style Chabad opened its doors in St. Augustine. A traditional Orthodox synagogue, Etz Chaim ("Tree of Life") is in the Mandarin area of nearby Jacksonville, a K-8 Jewish day school, Torah Academy of Jacksonville, is on the same property.[28]

Bonus joke: As the story goes, a Jewish man was found marooned for a long time on a deserted island. When he was eventually discovered, his rescuers noticed that he had built two synagogues on the island. They asked him why build two synagogues for just one guy? His answer: "Well, that's the one I go to; and the other is the one I would never go to."

Synagogue Dedication Ceremony, October 1923 [29]

A hand-written guide to who was who in that photo is shown below:

Corporate Name → Congregation Sons of Israel
Synagogue Dedication
May, 1923

1- Isaac Eff
2- Mrs. Isadore (Jennie) Feigenbaum
3- Mrs. M. L. (Anna) Pincus
4- M. L. Pincus
5- A. (Abe) Hamsey
6- A. R. (Abe) Friedman
7- Mrs. Morris (Libbie) Jaffe
8- ?
9- ? Mrs Harry [illegible] ??
10- Harry J. Eff
11- Mrs. Harry (Lena) Ross
12- Mrs. Mary (Friedman) Safer
13- Mrs. J. A. (Lena) Snyder
13A- Mrs. Jacob Zankinsky
14- Mrs. Morris (Esther) Friedman
15- Jack Wolfe
15A- Mrs. (Pearl) Jacob Wolfe
16- Mrs. D. Lestel
17- Mrs. J. A. Lew
18- Mamye (Snyder)
19-
20- [illegible] ??
21- Jennie (Jean) Hamee
22- Mrs. Morris Friedman
23- Max Friedman
24- Charles (Charlie) Weinberger
25- Max Jaffe
26- A. S. Weinstein

26 A - Mrs. A. S. Weinstein ??
27 Mrs. Isaac (Mirrel) Eff
27 A - Mrs. Ben Broudy
28 - Mrs. (Lena) David Price
29 - ? Weinstein ??
30 - Mrs. Rosa Gamse
30 A - ?
30 B - ?
30 C - Harry Gamse and child
31 - M. Kravitz
31 A - Mrs. M. Kravitz
32 - Mrs. Fannie (Abe) Gamsey
33 - Mrs. (A) Mamie (Gleitstein) (Eff) Rose
34 - Mrs. W. G. (Minnie) Pinkoson
34 A - Isadore Feigenbaum
35 - W. G. Pinkoson
35 A Sam Rincus
36 Sam Rose
37 Wexler
38 David Gross
38 A Mrs. David Gross
39 Wm. Rincus
40 A. Rose
41 Jacob Rose
41 A Jacob Tarlinsky
42 Harry Gamse
43 Harry Rose

44 S. A. Snyder
45 Julius Jaffe
46 Samuel Eff
47 Mrs. Max (Libbie) (Pinkerson) Jaffe
47A child
48 Abe Pinkerson
49 M. Knobloch
50 Mrs. [illegible]
51. Rebecca Butkowsky
52- Mrs. Keller
53 - ?
54- Rita Snyder ?
55- ?
56- ?

5. STAINED GLASS WINDOWS

The beautiful stained-glass windows in FCSI were designed by Joseph Llorens in 1873, and were originally part of the structure of synagogue Ahavath Achim ("Brotherly Love") in Atlanta. In the 1950s, this synagogue was in the way of the construction of interstate highways 75 and 85 and needed to be torn down and rebuilt elsewhere in Atlanta. The three daughters of FCSI founding leader Jacob Tarlinsky (Lena, Florence, and Sarah) learned about all this, traveled to Atlanta and arranged to purchase the windows, and ship them safely to St. Augustine, where they were installed in 1958. By the way, Florence Tarlinksy's marriage to Israel Freiden in 1924 was the occasion for the synagogue's first wedding ceremony (reported in the news clipping below). Mary Safer's, to her beloved Max, was the second, in 1926.[31]

Feiden-Tarlinsky Wedding Performed In New Synagogue

At 11 o'clock yesterday morning in the recently-completed Synagogue the wedding of Miss Florence Tarlinsky of this city and Israel Feiden, of Colchester, Conn., was quietly solemnized. Rev. M. Jaffee, who is in charge of the local Jewish congregation, performed the ceremony, and the bride was given in marriage by her father, Jacob Tarlinsky. It is interesting to note that this is the first wedding performed in the new Synagogue.

The bride was most attractive in a lovely frock of white georgette with trimmings of filet lace. Her veil of tulle was becomingly arranged under a wreath of lilies of the valley, and she carried an arm bouquet of bride's roses.

After the ceremony there was an informal reception in the social hall adjoining the synagogue, and later there was a family dinner at the Lorillard House, home of the bride's parents. The bride and groom left on the 12:40 p. m. train for New York where they will spend some time before going to their New England home. Mrs. Feiden is traveling in a modish coat suit of brown with hat scarf and other accessories to match.

Announcements which read as follows, have gone out today to the friends of Mr. and Mrs. Feiden and their families:

Mr. and Mrs. Jacob Tarlinsky
announce the marriage of
their daughter
Florence
to
Mr. Israel Feiden
October the twenty-sixth
One thousand, nine hundred and
twenty-four
St. Augustine, Florida.

At Home
after November fifth
One thousand nine hundred and
twenty-four
Colchester, Connecticut.

[32]

Fast forward to 2013, and during a Bar Mitzvah service, a man (from Gainesville, not a member of the congregation) got up from his seat and started staring upwards, in the direction of the stain-glass windows. Thinking that something was wrong, Les Stern went over to the man to ask why he was standing, as it was not a part of the service that necessitated getting up out of one's seat. Les asked the man, "Sir, are you alright?" He replied almost ominously, "I know those windows!"

At this point the man went into detail about how he had been a congregant at Ahavath Achim, and knew the great grandson of Joseph Llorens, who was still in the stained-glass artwork business. He commented that the glass had deteriorated and needed to be restored. At that point, FCSI contacted the great grandson, Charles Kenneth Hardeman, and arranged for the windows to be repaired, cleaned and reinforced.[33] Robert Lawrence remembers working together with Hardeman on the restoration project in St. Augustine, and has since taken over the Georgia-based business, which to this day is called "Llorens Stained Glass Studio & Hardeman Fine Art Glass." Hardeman, it turned out, still had his great-grandfather's drawings for these windows, so he and Lawrence could restore them back to the exact original designs without any guesswork.

Close-up showing Ark of the Covenant
(à la Indiana Jones, *Raiders of the Lost Ark*)

Center Window on North wall [34]

One final note relating to stained glass: When the original glass was installed back in 1958, there were some broken pieces. Some years later, during the synagogue's post-hurricane restoration (see chapter 8) local "mixed media" artist Wendy Mandel (neé McDaniel), created a beautiful mosaic design from those colorful glass shards. It can be seen over the main entry door to the synagogue, in and around the Star of David. She recalls that Les and Karen Stern came across the pieces of glass in some old desk drawers, and contacted the artist with the hope that she could create something out of them. The first idea was to intersperse the glass in the new concrete plaza, but that was unworkable, so Ms. McDaniel turned her focus to the space above the entry doors, and set to work on this project. She used 90 percent of the original glass, and in her words: "Wanted to reflect a sense of community .... for which the embodiment of peace and harmony is the Hebrew word Shalom." As you can see in the photo below, the word "Shalom" in Hebrew is surrounded by the swirling colors of the stained glass to create a very moving, artistic effect

Glass Mosaic Over Synagogue Entry Door [35]

6. THROUGH THE YEARS

According to an article in the Institute of Southern Jewish Life[36], St. Augustine's Jewish population grew to 91 families in the 1930s, with 41 members of FCSI serving in the U.S. armed forces in World War II. Branching out beyond the retail market business, St. Augustine Jews became more broadly represented in both the private and public sectors. Saul Snyder, for example, was a cattle rancher, whose land covered the area in and around what is currently the Cobblestone Village shopping plaza, just west of the intersection of Routes 1 and 312.

Jewish Cattle Rancher Saul P. Snyder [37]

Snyder's family background is itself a remarkable history, and is recounted in this post on the FCSI Facebook page, penned by Les Stern.

"Two young men, Solomon Schneiderman and Jacob Chosodovich, both from a small town near Kiev, immigrated to the United States in

1904. They made their way to Fernandina Beach where both got jobs in Goffin's oyster factory. Soon, their names had been changed to S.A. Snyder and Jacob Ross and both finally settled in St. Augustine where they established prosperous businesses. In 1906, Saul was able to send enough money to bring his wife to America, and she had a difficult and dangerous journey. It was not easy to cross the border into Germany even with papers, and Sarah had befriended another traveler, a young girl who had none. Determined to get past the frontier, the two women attempted to sneak across at night, but became separated in the dark. Sarah was caught by a Russian border guard who bludgeoned her with a rifle butt and stabbed her with the bayonet. Their next attempt, with the help of an agent who scattered around a few bribes, was successful, and soon Sarah had joined her husband in Fernandina Beach, where he was by then operating a small grocery store.

Mr. Tarlinsky, in St. Augustine, wrote that there was a need for two more Jewish men in order to establish the minyan (or 10 men) for services in the synagogue in the Oldest City. This prompted the move of Ross and Snyder to their new homes in 1907. Snyder opened his first grocery store in St. Augustine on Washington Street and soon journeyed to Jacksonville to buy a horse and wagon at the horse sales there. Since his family had raised cattle back in Russia, he picked out a good animal and so impressed the seller with his honesty and sagacity that he allowed him to take the outfit with no money down. He drove the horse and wagon back to St. Augustine and paid off the debt at the rate of $1 a week.

His next store was on Bridge Street, and finally, he moved his business to Granada Street, where it grew into one of the largest grocery stores in the city. In addition to his thriving grocery business, Snyder soon achieved his ambition of raising a herd of cattle as his family had done for generations. As noted above, his first ranch was in the area now occupied by the Cobblestone Village plaza. He later developed a big spread in an area near Bunnell. Snyder was instrumental in the formation of the St. Johns County Cattlemen's Association, and also became active in the nascent civic associations such as

Kiwanis Club, Legion of Honor and the Elks."[38]

Finally, Saul Snyder's daughter became the wife of Jerry Kass, a long-time influential member and president of the congregation, whose own biography is included below.

Another family that traces its roots to the early days is that of trustee Amy Galkin Capo. Amy's father, Joseph, remembers that his grandfather, Jacob Galkin, emigrated to the USA at the end of the 19th Century from Sevastopol, in the Crimea. He ran a clothing store in St. Augustine. Abraham Friedman, who married Belle Galkin, Jacob's daughter, became head of the Exchange Bank in St Augustine, currently doing business as "The Vault," a popular destination wedding venue.

Moving the way-back machine to May 8, 1955, we can see that a good number of congregants established the St. Augustine chapter of the Zionist Organization of America. The document is shown below[39]; not all the signatures are legible, but you can probably make out familiar FCSI surnames such as Lichter, Broudy, Bernstein, and Kass.

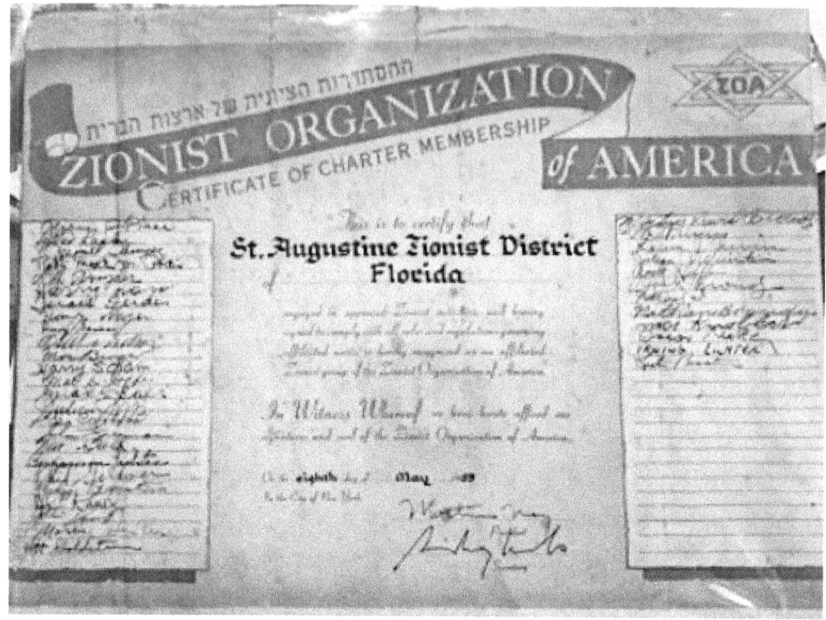

In March, 1979, FCSI honored Max Jaffe with a plaque, which was then hung on the newly renovated social hall, from that moment on to be named the Max Jaffe Hall (originally built in 1928). The ceremony noted Jaffe's 50 years of service to the congregation, which coincided with 50 years of his marriage to Libbie, to be celebrated a few months later. At this same March 1979 event, Nathan Weinstein, also awarded a commemorative plaque (for his long service as financial secretary), announced that his family would sponsor the building of another annex to the synagogue structure, which was finished in 1983. This was originally intended as a space for classrooms for a Hebrew school, named "Talmud Torah," but over time it has served as a kind of back stage for social events in the Max Jaffe Hall, complete with a restaurant-style kitchen. There simply has not been enough critical mass of youngsters to open a full-fledged Hebrew school; the few children who had to prepare for their Bar or Bat Mitzvah would do so privately with a rabbi or lay leader.

In 1980, the following form was submitted to register the synagogue with the Historic St. Augustine Preservation Board:

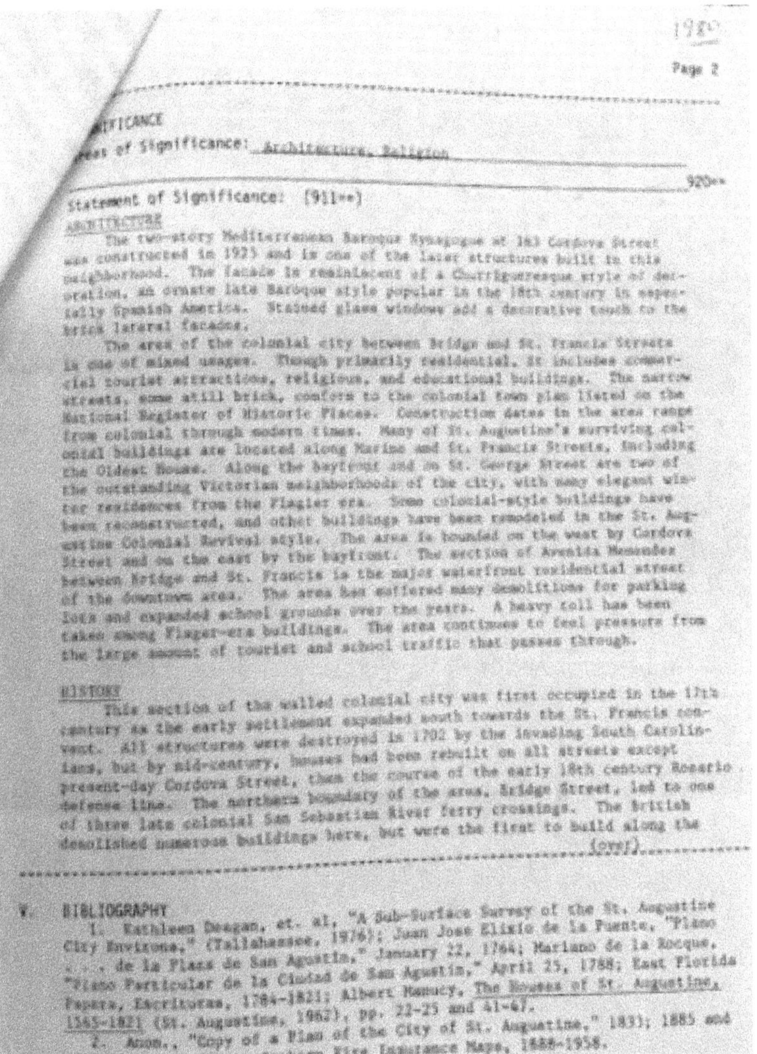

1980

Page 2

...IFICANCE

...eas of Significance: Architecture, Religion

920**

Statement of Significance: [911**]

ARCHITECTURE

The two-story Mediterranean Baroque Synagogue at 161 Cordova Street was constructed in 1923 and is one of the later structures built in this neighborhood. The facade is reminiscent of a Churrigueresque style of decoration, an ornate late Baroque style popular in the 18th century in especially Spanish America. Stained glass windows add a decorative touch to the brick lateral facades.

The area of the colonial city between Bridge and St. Francis Streets is one of mixed usages. Though primarily residential, it includes commercial tourist attractions, religious, and educational buildings. The narrow streets, some still brick, conform to the colonial town plan listed on the National Register of Historic Places. Construction dates in the area range from colonial through modern times. Many of St. Augustine's surviving colonial buildings are located along Marine and St. Francis Streets, including the Oldest House. Along the bayfront and on St. George Street are two of the outstanding Victorian neighborhoods of the city, with many elegant winter residences from the Flagler era. Some colonial-style buildings have been reconstructed, and other buildings have been remodeled in the St. Augustine Colonial Revival style. The area is bounded on the west by Cordova Street and on the east by the bayfront. The section of Avenida Menendez between Bridge and St. Francis is the major waterfront residential street of the downtown area. The area has suffered many demolitions for parking lots and expanded school grounds over the years. A heavy toll has been taken among Flagler-era buildings. The area continues to feel pressure from the large amount of tourist and school traffic that passes through.

HISTORY

This section of the walled colonial city was first occupied in the 17th century as the early settlement expanded south towards the St. Francis convent. All structures were destroyed in 1702 by the invading South Carolinians, but by mid-century, houses had been rebuilt on all streets except present-day Cordova Street, then the course of the early 18th century Rosario defense line. The northern boundary of the area, Bridge Street, led to one of three late colonial San Sebastian River ferry crossings. The British demolished numerous buildings here, but were the first to build along the

(over)

V. BIBLIOGRAPHY

1. Kathleen Deagan, et. al, "A Sub-Surface Survey of the St. Augustine City Environs," (Tallahassee, 1976); Juan Jose Elixio de la Puente, "Plano . . . de la Plaza de San Agustin," January 22, 1764; Mariano de la Rocque, "Plano Particular de la Ciudad de San Agustin," April 25, 1788; East Florida Papers, Escrituras, 1784-1821; Albert Manucy, The Houses of St. Augustine, 1565-1821 (St. Augustine, 1962), pp. 22-25 and 41-47.

2. Anon., "Copy of a Plan of the City of St. Augustine," 1833; 1885 and 1894 Birds-Eye Views; Sanborn Fire Insurance Maps, 1888-1958.

bayfront on the east side of Marine Street. The Spanish filled this low-lying land in the 1790's, and substantial residences were thereafter erected on the reclaimed land. The Spanish crown owned considerable property in this section of the colonial city, such as a school building near the south-east corner of Bridge and St. George Streets and the vacant land west of St. George Street where crops were raised by the garrison. Nine colonial buildings have survived in this section, particularly in clusters along Marine and St. Francis Streets: Sanchez, Marin, Puello, Jones and the two Rovira Houses on Marine; Tovar and Oldest House on St. Francis; and the St. Francis Inn on corner of St. George and St. Francis. The Llambias House and the St. Francis Barracks lie on the south side of St. Francis Street.(1) The area remained essentially residential throughout the American period, although several religious structures were built along St. George Street (the non-extant 19th century Presbyterian Church and the 20th century Cathedral Parish School complex) and along Cordova Street (the 20th century Synagogue). Several boarding houses were scattered throughout the area, most notably the St. Francis Inn building and the Valencia Hotel. Taken as a whole, this section has a high concentration of 18th and 19th century buildings on all streets except Cordova which was developed primarily in the 1920's.(2)

ARCHAEOLOGY

For archaeological significance of the walled colonial city see Master Site File Form 8SJ10.

Cornerstone laid May 3, 1923

[40]

Although that particular Historical Preservation Board was dissolved in 1997, the Synagogue's address appears on one of the downtown maps of the Historical Architectural Review Board, as well as on a tourist website providing a directory of historic churches in St. Augustine.[41]

The above image[42], depicting the installation of FCSI Board members in October, 1990, shows Marjorie Wyzan (upper row), who was the recording secretary at the time. Marjorie recently celebrated her 95th birthday and is still an active member of the synagogue in 2023. In the foreground are Max Jaffe (profiled in Chapter 7), and Jean Trapido-Rosenthal, who also served as the librarian of the St. Augustine Historical society in the 1980s. [43]

In March of 1999, inspectors from the Machon Ot (Institute of Letters) in New York visited the synagogue to carry out an inspection of its three Torah scrolls. Their verdict was that one of the three scrolls was in need of repair, which is not surprising, given that all three were brought to America in the 19th century. Machon Ot's bill was 3,500 dollars, which of course FCSI did not hesitate to pay.[44]

Although the craft of writing and assembling Torah scrolls goes back to antiquity, and the rules for writing and repairing them are the subject of commentaries by Talmudic scholars in the Middle Ages, Machon

Ot is a modern company, complete with a website: https://ott.co.il/torah-writing/ . If you visit there you can learn fascinating factoids such as:

- The Torah consists of 304,805 letters (Hebrew with no vowels);
- It takes a scribe, working five hours a day, a whole year to write a new Torah;
- The only observable divisions in the text are between the five books; otherwise, chapters and verses run one into the other.

The Torah is an object of great reverence to the Jewish people. When it is brought out from its ark (ritual cabinet) on the pulpit during a religious service, the whole congregation stands, and then takes turns touching it as it is walked around the sanctuary by whomever has the honor of holding it for that purpose. Rabbis are trained to know every chapter and verse, not only to read but also to interpret. The Torah contains 613 "Mitzvot," or commandments/instructions for the devout to follow. If nothing else, most of us are familiar ten of them, and maybe remember Charlton Heston (or Mel Brooks) coming down from Mt. Sinai holding the tablets on which they were etched in G_d's handwriting. As the prayer says when the Torah is returned to the ark: "It is a tree of life for those who hold fast to it; all who uphold it are blessed. Its ways are pleasant, and all its paths are peace."

Ark on the FCSI pulpit, holding the Torah Scrolls [45]

...*The Mystery of the Missing Candlestick*, by June Weltman provides a time-capsule view of St. Augustine and the synagogue at the turn of the 21st century. Although it is a work of young-adult fiction, the descriptions of the FCSI sanctuary and its history, as well as other well-known tourist attractions in the city, are all accurate. Additionally, some of the main characters are Jewish and members of the FCSI congregation.

Mystery of the Missing Candlestick
JUNE WELTMAN

Tu B'Shevat 2010

The image above[46] shows Rabbi Samuel Cywiak (profiled in Chapter 7) with Audrey Jacobson, a longtime FCSI member, planting a tree on the Jewish holiday "Tu B'Shevat," or Arbor Day in 2010. Audrey, who recently celebrated her 95th birthday at the synagogue, was once an Art Teacher at Weldon E. Howitt, Junior High School in Farmingdale, NY, and crossed paths with the author when he was a 9th-grader there in the 1969-70 academic year.[47]

7. LEADERS

Jerome "Jerry" Kass: Born in Jacksonville in 1914, Jerry Kass grew up in New York, and then returned to Florida/St. Augustine in 1933. He was a veteran of World War II, reaching the rank of Major in the U.S. Marine Corps. "Semper Fi." Mr. Kass and his wife, Rita, were in the grocery business. He also was a member of pretty much any and every civic association you could think of, for which he was awarded the "Order of La Florida," by the city of St. Augustine, which lowered flags to half-mast when he died in 2012. Jerry Kass was a devoted and active member of First Congregation Sons of Israel. He was FCSI president from 1990-95.[48] Despite all the above, Jerry Kass may be best known for his volunteer gig as broadcaster of St. Augustine High School football games. His son, Barry, carried on that tradition until he himself retired from the job in 2021.[49]

JERRY KASS, 89, has lived in St. Augustine nearly his whole life and has documented the history of the Jewish community buried at the Sons of Israel Cemetery on Evergreen Street. Today, he is the only person from the congregation to have a plan for all of the grave plots in the cemetery. The cemetery offers free plots to all members of the Congregation Sons of Israel, which was formed in St. Augustine around 1898. **Photos by JUSTIN YURKANIN,**

Jerry Kass at the Cemetery gates, January 2004 [50]

<u>Max Jaffe:</u> Born in Polisk, Poland in 1902, Max Jaffe moved to St. Augustine in 1925 and lived there until his passing, just shy of his 105th birthday in April, 2007. His wife, Libbie, was the daughter of Arthur Pinkoson, who was married to Jacob Tarlinsky's sister. During Max's long life he was one of the most beloved members of the congregation, often serving as a lay leader of religious services, a member and officer on the Board of Trustees, and always contributing funds above and beyond the call of dues or duty. The social hall annex behind the FCIS sanctuary is aptly named the Max and Libbie Jaffe Hall. His obituary recalls his sense of humor: When asked what was the secret to a long

life, he said "Eat the right food and drink schnapps." Jaffe was in the grocery-food business and also motels. Beyond the synagogue he was involved with other civic associations such as the Rotary Club, Shriners, and Freemasons. Max's son, Larry Jaffe, would continue the family tradition as significant donor to FCSI, and as cantor and lay leader, remembered especially for his singing voice.

Max Jaffe[51]

The image below shows these two FCSI stalwarts, Max Jaffe and Jerry Kass, holding the Torah scrolls at the beginning of High Holy Day services in 1987.

Max Jaffe and Jerry Kass in 1987 [52]

The Tarlinsky Family Tree:

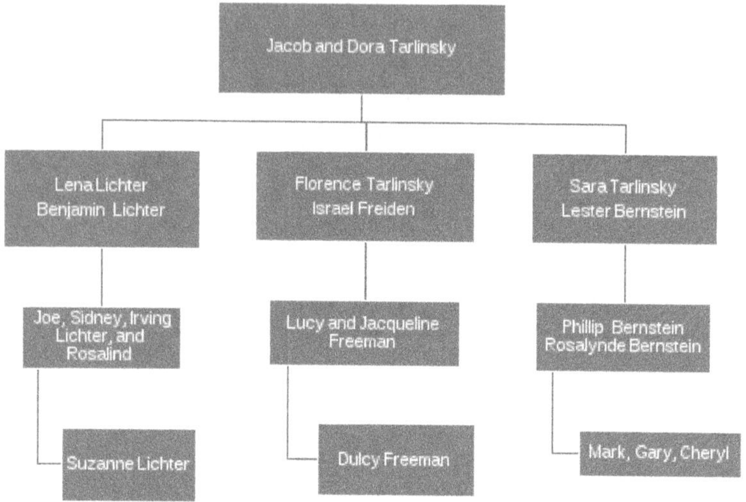

Multiple Tarlinsky Descendants: Florence, Lena and Sarah at left[53]

The above photo may be the only one available that shows the three daughters of Jacob and Dora Tarlinsky. It was taken at Sarah's oldest grandson's bris (ritual circumcision)[54] in February, 1951. Left to right - Florence Feiden, Lena Lichter and Sarah Bernstein. Rosalind Bernstein Baumstein and her husband Jack are next. Suzanne Lichter's aunt Mimi married to her uncle Mitchell Baumstein, sitting with young Barry in his lap are next. Standing next to Mimi is Harry (Zvi) Baumstein and his second wife Rebecca. Rebecca was a holocaust survivor and a childhood friend of Harry's in Romania. Harry's first wife (also Rebecca) died before the war, and after the war Rebecca 2 reached out to Harry from a displaced persons camp. He brought her to Cuba, where they married in 1948. Seated in front of her is Sidney (Buddy) Lichter.

Suzanne Lichter[55]: In the FCSI leadership transition in the Fall of 2023, Suzanne has stepped forward to take on the position of Treasurer, a position for which she is eminently qualified as a retired career accountant. Suzanne nowadays serves as a volunteer at the River Garden retirement home in Jacksonville. As you can see above in the (admittedly incomplete) family tree, Suzanne is the great-grand-daughter of Jacob and Dora Tarlinsky, and very proud of her St. Augustine Jewish community lineage. In addition to the Tarlinsky bloodlines, her other ancestry goes back to Poland and Romania. As an adolescent, the Romanian, Herb Zvi Baumstein, saw bad times coming and first tried to escape to the New World as a stowaway on a boat departing from Spain in 1910. He was caught, but then tried again with a sponsoring family, the Rosenbergs in New York, and was successful. He married Rosenberg's daughter, Rebecca, then later moved to Lake City, Florida to open up a retail business. Suzanne was born in Gainesville, and moved eventually to Jacksonville. She provided a wealth of information for this book by way of an oral interview, as well as some documents and photographs. Very significantly, she and her aunt Rosalind made a sizeable financial contribution to underwrite the renovation of the Max and Libbie Jaffe Hall, which was severely damaged by Hurricane Irma in 2017. That donation is immortalized by lettering over the entrance to the main sanctuary that honors her grandparents, Benjamin and Lena Lichter.

Benjamin Lichter: Benjamin, born in 1887, grew up in New York (see school photo), and became the son-in-law of Jacob Tarlinsky upon his marriage to Lena, on November 23, 1914. Two of many congratulatory telegrams to the newlywed couple are shown below. Additionally, in the display case image, you can see a photo of Lena, a vase presented to the newlyweds as a present from FCSI members, and Lena's thank-you note back to the congregation, written in Yiddish. Benjamin's marriage to Lena got him into the Tarlinsky family's slipper manufacturing business in New York, until the facility was burned down in union-organized violence in 1936. That was the proximate cause for his move down to Florida. He eventually served as president of the congregation, as well as cantor. And, like so many others in the St. Augustine Jewish community, opened up a retail clothing store on St. George Street, initially called "Benjamin's." This was on property originally purchased by his mother-in-law, Dora.

Young Benjamin Lichter (front/middle) at PS 101 in New York, Circa 1900[56]

WESTERN UNION
TELEGRAM

RECEIVED AT 250 Broadway, Brooklyn, N. Y.

[illegible] CH 19 [illegible]

ST AUGUSTINE FLO NOV 23RD-14.

MR AND MRS BENJ LICTHER.

ACCEPT MY HEARTY CONGRATULATIONS [illegible] TO BE WILL BE SHIP AHOY

HAPPINESS AND BEST JOY EVERYBODY ST AUGUSTINE WISHES YOU WELL .

MAX D [illegible].

645 P.M.

WESTERN UNION
TELEGRAM

RECEIVED AT 250 Broadway, Brooklyn, N. Y.

70NY CH. 24 [illegible]

ST AUGUSTINE FLO NOV 23RD-1914.

MR AND MRS BENJ LICHTER,

HERES WISHING YOU WHAT YOU DESIRE IN HONOR OF THE

DAY MAY FORTUNATE AND HAPPINESS LEFT YOU SOEH HIGHER AND

EVER BY YOU STAY.

ISIDORE FEIGENBAUM.

55P.M.

Lichter Marriage Congrats and display case[57]

Phillip Bernstein: In the 2007 edition of the St. Augustine Journal of History, "El Escribano," Phillip Bernstein (1926-2015) penned his memoirs from his childhood growing up in St. Augustine.[58] Besides his recollections of religious services during FCSI's Orthodox era and its changeover to Conservative, he also wrote about his Americana experiences playing football and basketball for Ketterlinus High School. As an adult, in addition to his devotion to the synagogue, including his (1980's) service as president, he was a successful businessman: Owner of J.R. Department store downtown, and a surf shop in St. Augustine Beach.

Phillip Bernstein[59]

Rabbi Cywiak: Samuel Cywiak, originally from Wyszkow, Poland, became Rabbi at FCSI in 1992. This ended a period of roughly 30 years during which time the synagogue had no permanent rabbi. Cywiak's life was launched into high drama as he was the lone survivor of a Nazi mass execution of Jews in his hometown in 1939. He escaped to Soviet Russia, and then, after suffering extraordinary hardships, managed to emigrate to the USA in 1947. Rabbi Cywiak would often give public lectures on the Holocaust, and wrote a book about his life experiences entitled *Flight From Fear*.

He served as rabbi in Louisville, KY and Jersey City, NJ, before moving to Venezuela to serve as Rabbi for the Israeli Union of Caracas. There he married Venezuelan congregant Rukmini, who moved with him to St. Augustine. He and Rukmini were fortunate to have left Venezuela before the rule of Hugo Chavez, who was very hostile to Israel and to the Caracas Jewish community. During that time, according to the Latin America Jewish grapevine, Caracas Jews, regardless of their ethnicity, stopped using the Yiddish/Ashkenazi Sabbath greeting "Güt Shabbos," because it sounded too much like "Good Chavez." Instead they went with the Sephardic Hebrew greeting "Shabbat Shalom."

Rabbi Cywiak's tenure at FCSI lasted until 2011, making him the longest-serving rabbi FCSI ever had. Rabbi Cywiak's training was very old-school, Orthodox, but he was happy to embrace the Conservative egalitarian style of FCSI. He passed away in Miami in 2013 at the age of 93.[60]

1998 Rosh Hashana services: Martin Broudy and Rabbi Cywiak[61]

The Broudys:

The Patriarch of the Broudy family was Benjamin Broudy, who first landed in Boston in the early 20th century, emigrating from Poland, via what was then called Palestine. He met and married Rose Broudy, who had immigrated from Lithuania in 1903. The first two of their three sons were born in Boston: Nathan and Jack. They moved to St. Augustine in 1922 (joining Benjamin's sister Annie and her husband Abe, who were already settled there) and soon afterwards had their third son, Martin Broudy, nicknamed "Baby." Benjamin and Rose first had a milk depot on St. George Street, and then opened up one grocery store on Spanish Street, and another on King Street.

1922 photo of Benjamin and Rose Broudy, with sons

Nathan and Jack flanking "Baby" Martin[62]

The King Street grocery store, shown below[63], became a partnership of the three next-gen Broudy sons, which included a liquor section (after Prohibition was repealed in 1933). Martin subsequently made liquor retailing (Jews with the booze) a separate business and expanded it with stores throughout St. Augustine and as far north as Jacksonville.

He served as president of First Congregation Sons of Israel for 20 years. The Broudy family has, over the years, been one of the largest financial donors and sponsors of FCSI, a tradition continued to the third generation, with Martin's children Barry and Joan serving as board members and officers.

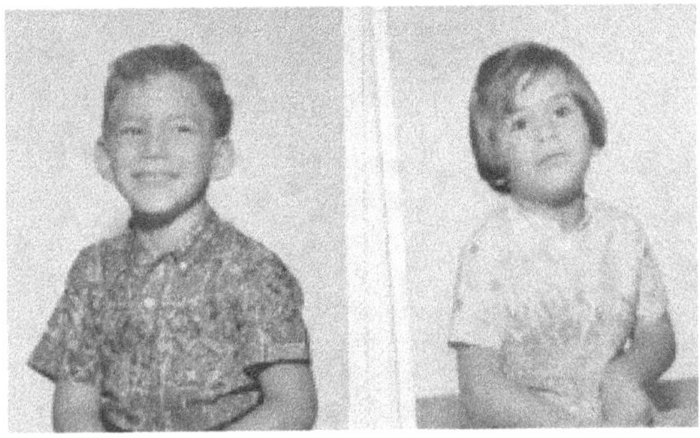

Barry and Joan Broudy in their youth[64]

Barry has also been, for many years, the honored sounder of the Shofar, or ram's horn, to usher in the Jewish New Year during Rosh Hashana services. In recent years he has been joined by Steve Pollack, creating a dramatic "dueling Shofars" performance of great skill and reverence. It is fitting that in this centennial year, Barry has been elected president of the congregation, and Joan a returning board member as recording secretary.

Their cousin, Simone Broudy-Kilbourn, a retired guidance counselor and mental health professional, has amassed a wealth of historical information about FCSI. She shared that with the author, and also did an oral interview at her home in North Vilano Beach. Simone is the daughter of Nathan Broudy and Evelyn Love Comick Broudy. Evelyn's father, Sam Comick, an itinerant peddler, and his wife, Lena, had settled in Palatka in 1908, then moved soon afterwards to St. Augustine. Evelyn had a degree from NYU and worked for the New York Times. Visiting St. Augustine, she met Nathan Broudy at the family grocery store, and came back from New York to marry him in

1947. She earned a business degree from Florida State and then taught business courses in the St. Johns County school system.

A Youthful Simone Broudy-Kilbourn[65]

<u>The Sterns</u>:

With his salt-and-pepper beard, penetrating eyes, and operatic baritone voice, Les Stern cuts an impressive figure. He served for 14 years as president of the FCSI congregation, finally stepping down after the High Holy Days services in the Fall of 2023. His initial term began in 2009, when, as Second Vice-President, he fell into the top job after both the President and First Vice President both resigned. Since then, he has been returned to the office for each successive term by popular election of the membership. He is a font of wisdom regarding FSCI history, and provided a fair amount of the material for this book by way of an oral interview. He was born in 1947 in Cleveland, Ohio, and came to St. Augustine from Ohio in 1973, following his father's migration south many years earlier. Les was first a teacher, and then, after providing some training to the St. Johns County Sheriff's office, became a law enforcement officer himself. Les Stern's "running mate" on the Board of Directors is his wife, Karen Stern, who has been treasurer during that extended period. Karen is originally from Alabama, and met Les in St. Augustine, while she was working for Barnett Bank. She has since served as a County Commissioner in St. Johns County, and is about as resourceful as resourceful gets.

Les and Karen Stern [66]

Rene Naughton:

Rene (photo appears in Chapter 8) has been an FCSI Board member for four years, and in the new fiscal year, which began in September,

2023, was elected vice-president. She is from a long line of synagogue members, dating back to her great-grandmother, and her grandmother, Esther Wexler, who came to the United States at age eight. Rene's parents were Rosalie and Max Kaplan. Max owned a bar in the West King Street neighborhood, appropriately named "Mac's Bar." On her mother's side, grandfather Jack Wexler, who fought in the U.S. Army in World War I, would drive his truck every Friday evening to Jacksonville, pick up the Jewish servicemembers at Jacksonville military bases, and bring them to St. Augustine for religious services, and to spend the weekend with local Jewish families. One of those military guys was Max Kaplan, which was how he met Rosalie.

Rene spent her childhood in St. Augustine, and remembers how all the Jewish families were clustered together in the area near the synagogue, and how they spent so much time there. In her own case, most of the weekdays in religious/Hebrew school (with then-Rabbi Silverman), plus Friday evening Sabbath services. Rene also has happy memories of Black-Jewish relationships from that time period, consistent with the research project cited in Chapter 2 about businesses in the Lincolnville neighborhood (starting just West of Cordova Street), which is in the National Register of Historic Places. As a young adult, Rene went off to the University of Florida to get a degree in Education. She moved to Orlando, where she met her husband, Peter, then subsequently moved back to St. Augustine, where she has lived ever since. Over her 34-year professional career she has taught at every level, from Kindergarten through college, plus teaching religious school at the Bet Yam synagogue.[67]

Wedding Ceremony of Rene Naughton's Aunt/Uncle, 1947[68]

Reggie Daniels

Reginald Daniels[69] became a member of the congregation in 2008, on the occasion of his conversion to Judaism, under the guidance of Rabbi Cywiak. His deep understanding of holy scripture was what motivated him to become part of "Am Yisrael," (The Jewish people), and he brought along his wife, Eleah, and their children and grandchildren. Over the years he developed a close affinity with Rabbi Cywiak, and also with FCSI President Les. Stern. Originally from St. Petersburg, he grew up in the Gainesville area, and then enlisted in the U.S. Army. His assignments took him to Germany, and then Washington State, where, after his honorable discharge, he studied both mechanical engineering and the construction trades. Reggie, now a Board member for many years, has volunteered those skills for many projects to improve FCSI, most notably, the rebuilding of the wooden railing along the ramp from the sanctuary to the social hall, and the reinstallation and upgrades to the memorial plaque wall. He also builds the ceremonial pavilion ("Sukkah") each year for the annual Fall harvest festival holiday "Sukkot."

Reggie Daniels (right) Overseeing Repair of Memorial Plaque Board – August 2023[70]

8. STORM DAMAGE

In October 2016, Hurricane Matthew caused extensive damage to Saint Augustine, as it followed a northward path just off Florida's Atlantic coast. At that point it was a Category 3 storm, which is severe enough; during its trajectory through the Caribbean it had reached Category 5, the maximum level on the Simpson-Saffir scale.

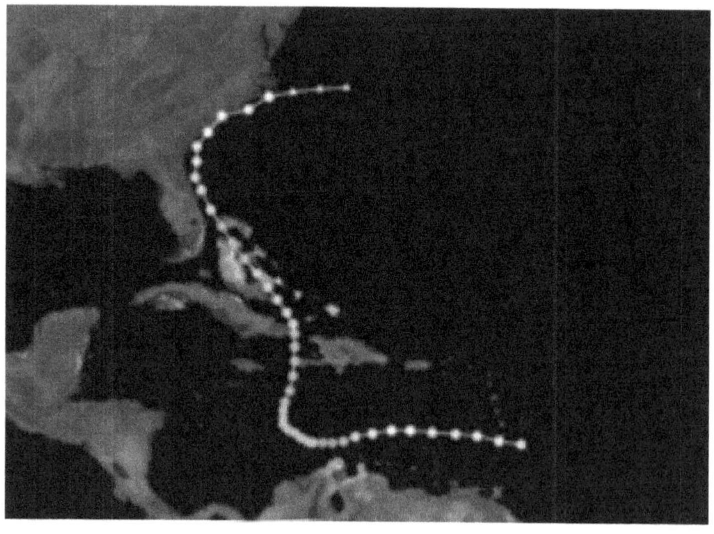

Path of Hurricane Matthew [71]

Late on the night of October 7, Karen Stern received a call from the St. Augustine Police Department with the news that water was gushing out of the front doors of the synagogue, and also lapping up at the back doors. Cordova Street, before St. Augustine's Flagler-financed urban expansion in the 19th Century, had been a creek. Hurricane Matthew caused so much flooding in the downtown area, that the street essentially reverted to its creek origins, with water flowing from north to south, emptying out into Maria Sanchez Lake.

With a green light from the police to go to the synagogue early the next morning, Les and Karen Stern made their way downtown to check out the damage. Upon entering the building, they found 12 or more inches of water in the sanctuary. Starting from the back, they waded through the shin-deep water, and made their way to what had been the rabbi's study near the front of the building. Forcing the door to that room open, they were hit with a heavy rush of water, that included office equipment, supplies, and files in the flotsam and jetsam that poured out of the room.

Les contacted the damage restoration company ServPro, urging them to come that same day to pump the water out. It was a Saturday, meaning a Sabbath day, but the urgency of the situation required bending of the rules of what one can and cannot do on Shabbat. ServPro people responded to the call and pumped all the water out. Then it was possible to assess the extent of the damage. As it turned out, floors, walls and seats were all ruined by the water, requiring extensive repairs. Karen Stern launched a fundraising campaign that was able to raise 450,000 dollars, which included a loan from the Small Business Administration. It took almost two years to get the synagogue ready to be used again, culminating in a much-heralded re-opening ceremony in May of 2018. In between, Florida was gob-smacked again by Hurricane Irma, which caused heavy water damage to the two annex buildings: The Weinstein Talmud Torah wing, and the Max Jaffe Hall.

Representatives of the Federal Emergency Management Administration (FEMA) came onto the scene and essentially mandated that the synagogue create a stronger barrier between the front of the building and Cordova Street. One component was to build a small, raised plaza, which would move the front steps a few yards away from the building. Additionally, FCSI needed to replace the damaged, wooden front doors with a heavier set of metal doors, which cost 12,000 dollars to purchase and install.

The FEMA inspection also revealed irreparable damage to the walls on the north and south sides of the building, below the large stained-glass windows. Layers of ruined wood and plasterboard were removed, revealing the underlying brick structure, which was intact. Rather than reinstall new wood or plasterboard, the synagogue leadership opted to leave the brickwork exposed, and apply a sealant to the surface. This is an attractive effect (see photo), which also exposes black conduits that were originally pipes through which natural gas flowed as the source for the building's first generation of lights. The sconces above each of those conduits are, of course, powered nowadays by electricity, but with the pipes exposed it is not hard to imagine the gas lights of a hundred years ago. One additional note on lighting: Up above in the balcony seating area, the original lighting was large wax candles, supported by shelves that came out from the walls.

Stain Glass Windows, Brickwork, and Gas Conduit[72]

One final aspect of the post-hurricane repairs was to replace the sanctuary's central chandelier. Before that could be done, Flagler College Art History graduate Liz Burris became involved and convinced the FCSI leadership that a giant Star of David should be installed on the ceiling, above the new chandelier. Burris researched the history of Eastern European synagogues to come up with a design for the gilded six-sided star and also took part in its physical installation (see photos below), with help from fellow Flagler College alums Mason Mushunski and John Roberts.[73]

Installing the New Star of David Finished Product

When all the work was done, the synagogue held a gala reopening celebration on the weekend of August 24-26, 2018. Here below is the invitation:

Additionally, the reopening made a splash in the local media. The image below shows the beginning of an article in the St. Augustine Record, with a wonderful photo of Board member Rene Naughton looking down on the sanctuary from the balcony level.[74]

8/24/18

Damaged by multiple hurricanes, synagogue ready for next chapter

By Anne C. Heymen
Correspondent

Gabriel "Gabe" Naughton, now 15, had no idea that when he participated in his Bar Mitzvah in August 2016 that he would be adding to the religious history of his family as the fifth generation to have close ties with St. Augustine's First Congregation Sons of Israel.

As it turned out, Gabe's celebration, which declared him a full-fledged member of the Jewish community, was the last solemn ceremony to be held in the sanctuary at 161 Cordova St., where the first service was held March 30, 1924. Just two months later, the synagogue was ravaged by Hurricane Matthew, which pounded the city in October 2016.

Less than a year later, in September 2017, Hurricane Irma hit the East Coast and added further destruction to an already damaged structure.

See READY, A5

Reopening celebration

Where: First Congregation Sons of Israel, 161 Cordova St.
Info: 904-829-9532, FCSI1924@gmail.com
Today: Ribbon cutting, 4-6 p.m.; Wine & Cheese tours, 5-6 p.m.
Saturday: Reception & Silent Auction, 6-8 p.m.; Historic Overview/Musical Gala, 8-10 p.m.
Sunday: Tours of Historic Sanctuary, noon to 3 p.m.

First Congregation Sons of Israel board member Rene Naughton stands on the balcony of the historic synagogue in St. Augustine on Thursday. Five generations of Naughton's family have worshiped at the synagogue on Cordova Street. Starting today, a three-day gala — "Restoring Our Past, Building Our Future" — will herald the completion of the first phase of an ongoing renovation of the synagogue following damage from hurricanes Matthew and Irma.
[PETER WILLOTT/THE RECORD]

9. SECURITY

St. Augustine is a city that has gone from extremes of tolerance to ethnic tension in its storied history. During the Spanish colonial period, slaves who escaped from English territories and made their way into Florida were accepted as free men—in exchange for conversion to Catholicism and service in the Spanish militia. Their training and exercises were held at Fort Mose, on the north side of the city, currently a Florida State historical site, very much linked to Castillo San Marcos. In fact, during the 1740 siege of St. Augustine by the British, soldiers from Fort Mose joined forces successfully with the Spanish garrison at Castillo San Marcos to repel the invaders.

Modern-Day Reenactors at Fort Mose[75]

On the other extreme, St. Augustine was the scene of violent racial tension in the early 1960s, bringing Martin Luther King Jr. and other civil rights leaders to the city to protest against segregation and exclusion of African Americans from public facilities. Dr. King was arrested, and from his jail cell appealed for outside help, which came in the form of a contingent of 16 Reform rabbis from the Northeast who protested on Dr. King's behalf and against segregated facilities. The rabbis were themselves arrested, which went down in American history as the largest arrest ever of rabbis. The St. Augustine Jewish Historical Society devotes considerable effort to commemorating this event, particularly the role of the visiting rabbis.[76]

Nowadays, Saint Augustine has swung back to toleration, which besides being moral, ethical and lawful, is appropriate for a city seeking to welcome as many tourists as possible from pretty much everywhere. And FCSI itself has a diverse membership, including an African-American member of the Board of Trustees.

...After the deadly attack on the Tree of Life synagogue in Pittsburgh, in October 2018, which killed 11 and wounded 6 worshippers during a Saturday morning Sabbath service, FCSI convened a meeting to address synagogue security. A security committee met among themselves, then had a follow up session with representatives of the local fire and police departments. Following their recommendations, FCSI installed a security camera at the entrance door, and instituted a procedure whereby entrance to the building would require a visual identification. It was not a problem for members, as the numbers are relatively small and most congregants know, or at least recognize each other. On the other hand, this being Saint Augustine, all kinds of visitors could show up, including Jewish tourists who just want to join a worship service. They would be subject to a short, polite Q and A before being let in.

For High Holy Day observances (Rosh Hashana and Yom Kippur), when much larger numbers of congregants are in attendance, an armed law-enforcement agent would stand guard at the entry to the building, with his/her marked police car very visible in the parking lot. At other times, police can and will respond promptly to a call reporting any suspicious activity at or near the synagogue. According to Les Stern, St. Augustine police records only reported one overt anti-Semitic attack against the synagogue in its history, which was the painting of a swastika on the building, sometime in the late 1940s.[77] That said, the congregation remains committed to taking security very seriously, not falling prey to the attitude that "It could never happen here."

The heightened security measures adopted in 2018 seemed to be working well, without any objections by the membership, when it all became a moot point in the wake of the Coronavirus pandemic in early 2020. At that point the synagogue closed its doors, and conducted religious services virtually, using the "Zoom" application on computers and portable devices. The synagogue resumed with hybrid services in 2021, that is, in-person in the sanctuary, but also broadcast on Zoom for those who wish to observe remotely.

10. THE SYNAGOGUE TODAY

As Jewish year 5784 begins in the Fall of 2023, First Congregation Sons of Israel is undergoing a leadership transition, as noted in the introductory section. The newly installed Board of Directors and key officers are every bit as committed to "keeping the lights on," and continuing FCSI's traditions as have the Boards that preceded it. It is a constant challenge, but is not new to FCSI, as the size of the congregation has had its peaks and valleys over its 115-year existence (counting from the 1908 incorporation document). There are currently roughly 50 "membership units," which can be families or individuals, a slight increase from a few years before, but still a small number. Most will have shown up for Rosh Hashana and Yom Kippur, but during the rest of the year, the congregation will struggle to assemble a minyan (ten adults) for each weekly Sabbath service.

My father, Arthur Blau, who was a congregant from 1992 until he died in 2006 (and is buried in the cemetery) used to quip that "The average age of the FCSI congregation is....deceased." It is still hard not to notice presently, that most of the members are late middle age or older, and that children are few and far between. In part that is a function of St. Augustine's overall demographics, which reflect the fact that it is a haven for retirees. Another factor within the Jewish world is that while the Orthodox tend to be fruitful and multiply, Conservative and Reform Jews have fewer children. Orthodox Etz Chaim, in Jacksonville, by contrast, is teeming with children. With these demographics in mind, it is (painfully) much more common for FCSI to schedule a funeral than a Bar or Bat Mitzvah.

The small membership presents a challenge, and a kind of Catch-22 regarding retaining the services of a full-time Rabbi. That is, over time, the presence of a full-time Rabbi would be a magnet for new members;

but in the short term, there are not enough dues-paying members for FCSI to be able to afford to sign a contract with such a Rabbi. The solution has been to invite guest Rabbis to officiate on an intermittent basis.

Currently FCSI has two such visiting Rabbis that lead religious services at a minimum of once every three weeks, and sometimes as frequently as twice a month. The two of them are highly esteemed and adored by the congregation, and are about as different from one another as could possibly be.

Rabbi Joel Fox was born and raised in Dallas, then moved with his family to Jerusalem as an adolescent. He was first trained as a cantor, and then fully ordained as a rabbi in 2013. He became the rabbi for Temple Beth Sholom in Melbourne, Florida in 2014. He left that position in 2017, and crossed paths with Les Stern when presiding over a funeral in St. Augustine. At that point he was available to be a part-time rabbi for FCSI, in addition to performing Jewish weddings in a wide geographical area. Rabbi Fox has been married to Natalia "Tali" for 26 years; they have three children: Adrianna, Daniella, and Michael.

Rabbi Joel Fox [78]

Rabbi Fox is all energy and excitement. He usually brings an electronic keyboard to the synagogue and performs a running musical accompaniment to his own booming singing voice that fills up the building as though it were Carnegie Hall. His style combines deep knowledge of Torah and the Hebrew language, the latter in part a function of his having lived in Israel and served in the Israeli Defense Forces. He uses the pulpit to teach as much as to pray, imparting as much information and wisdom as he can possibly fit into a two-hour service. He is also hilariously funny, and keyed into popular cultural and other trends. For example, when congregants are called up for an "Aliyah[79]," that is, to bless the Torah before and after the Rabbi reads each segment of the weekly portion ("Par'sha"), he compares the place they stand afterwards to the converse of a baseball on-deck circle. That is, the honoree does the blessings to the Rabbi's right, then moves to the Rabbi's left while the next honoree takes his turn "at bat." At times he uses Beatles song-melodies as the accompaniment to prayers. A participant in a Rabbi Fox service will be guaranteed to come away both educated and entertained.

Rabbi Mona Decker, originally from Silver Spring, Maryland, moved to Jacksonville in 2005. In between, she remembers strong childhood influences from her family's Conservative synagogue and from B'nai B'rith Youth. After obtaining a degree in Psychology from the University of Maryland, she went off to Israel for her first of two six-month stays, living each time on a Kibbutz, and studying Hebrew in the "Ulpan" immersion course. She next spent a number of years working for a home health care company, before enrolling in the Reconstructionist Rabbinical College in 1990. Soon after completing her studies and becoming ordained, she became the pulpit rabbi at the Bolton Street Synagogue in Baltimore. Her recollection of that period highlights the warmth and inclusivity of the congregation.

After she resettled in Jacksonville, Rabbi Decker worked as Chaplain for Community Hospice in the Northeast Florida area, which included Saint Augustine. In that capacity, she met FCSI President Les Stern, who arranged to have her preside over Martin Broudy's funeral in 2012. From then on, she officiated at other funerals and miscellaneous religious ceremonies for FCSI members, and eventually led a Sabbath Service in 2016. In 2021, Les Stern, with Board approval, invited Rabbi Decker to be part of the regular rotation of visiting rabbis. She said she feels "honored and privileged to be part of this synagogue's history and traditions," doing her part to keep the congregation active and engaged. She enjoys facing new challenges, such as having to improvise a Sukkot[80] service in the FCSI parking lot under a makeshift tent during the recent COVID pandemic.[81]

Rabbi Decker is soft-spoken and un-self-assuming. Her style is to pull up a chair just below the pulpit and lead the service as though it were a Socratic-method graduate school seminar. She does painstaking research in preparation for each service, usually bringing paper handouts with materials that supplement what we have in our regular prayer-books. Like Rabbi Fox, Rabbi Decker makes a concerted effort to educate the congregation on interpretations of the weekly Torah portion, usually seeking to apply their relevance to issues of the modern day. She will often add recorded music to services she leads, while also chanting in Hebrew with a mellifluous singing voice.

Rabbi Mona Decker[82]

In between the appearances of the visiting rabbis, FCSI maintains a schedule of Friday evening and Saturday morning Sabbath services presided over by lay leaders. Currently the regular rotation includes Robert Gerson, Robert Schachter, and Frank Wiener. Their dedication, adherence to the rituals, as well as their Hebrew reading skills, are an inspiration to the congregants who attend those services.

A good news story that may coincide within a few months of this book's release is the re-opening of the Max and Libbie Jaffe Social Hall, which was severely damaged by Hurricane Irma in 2017. This will provide a space for the weekly "Oneg Shabbat," or informal, typically catered gathering of congregants after the ritual Sabbath service concludes. As before, Passover Seders, meetings, and maybe even wedding or Bar/Bat Mitzvah receptions can be expected to fill up the social hall. Additionally, community events of a non-religious nature can also be invited to use the hall (for a reasonable fee); which can have the effect of attracting new members.

11. CONCLUSION

The origins and trajectory of the Jewish community in St. Augustine is in many ways a microcosm of the overall Jewish experience in the United States. The founding families arrived as immigrants in the late 19th or early 20th centuries, during what was by far the largest wave of Jewish immigration to America. They were pushed out of Czarist Russia and Eastern Europe by poverty and/or violent persecution, and pulled in by the lure of religious freedom and great economic opportunity. Their success says a lot about both themselves and about the country that took them in, which for Jews has most certainly been a land of opportunity. In the matrix below, you can see the history of the Jewish population in the United States over the years:

Year	Jewish Population	Year	Jewish Population
1654	25	1937	4,641,000-4,831,180
1700	200-300	1940	4,770,000-4,975,000
1776	1,000-2,500	1950	4,500,000-5,000,000
1790	1,243-3,000	1960	5,367,000-5,531,500
1800	2,000-2,500	1970	5,370,000-6,000,000
1820	2,650-5,000	1980	5,500,000-5,920,890
1826	6,000	1992	5,828,000
1830	4,000-6,000	2009	6,544,000
1840	15,000	2011	6,588,065
1848	50,000	2012	6,721,680
1850	50,000-100,000	2013	6,721,965
1860	150,000-200,000	2014	6,769,000
1870	200,000	2015	7,160,000
1880	230,000-280,000	2016	6,856,304
1890	400,000-475,000	2017	6,850,865
1900	937,800-1,058,135	2018	6,925,475
1910	1,508,000-2,349,754	2019	6,968,600
1920	3,300,000-3,604,580	2020	7,153,065
1927	4,228,029	2021	7,300,000
		2022	7,387,992

Virtual Jewish Library: Jewish Population of the United States [83]

Of the current total, about ten percent live in Florida, putting the state in third place behind New York and California.

Although incidents of anti-Semitism are most newsworthy, and certainly threatening to Jews in America, the biggest threats are spiritual and demographic. As is the case among followers of the major American Christian churches, more and more younger Jews drift away from participating in organized religion. Not to mention that low fertility rates and intermarriage are already eating away at the numbers of Jews in the next generation. The graphic below, from the Pew Research Center[84], shows the relatively low levels of observance among today's Jewish population. Note that it includes a demographic category named "Jews of no religion," that is, people of Jewish origin who do not practice the religion.

People of Jewish affinity and background rarely attend synagogue, but many go to non-Jewish services and say religion is important to them

	NET Jewish	Jews by religion	Jews of no religion	Jewish background	Jewish affinity
Synagogue attendance	%	%	%	%	%
Weekly or more	12	16	<1	4	4
Monthly/yearly	35	45	8	10	9
Seldom/never	52	38	91	85	75
No answer	1	1	<1	1	11
	100	100	100	100	100
Held or attended Seder last Passover					
Yes	62	74	30	22	17
No	37	25	70	76	71
No answer	1	1	<1	1	12
	100	100	100	100	100
Non-Jewish religious service attendance					
Weekly or more	2	3	<1	18	26
Monthly/yearly	11	13	8	22	14
Seldom/never	86	83	92	59	50
No answer	1	1	<1	1	11
	100	100	100	100	100
Importance of religion					
Very important	21	28	2	35	49
Somewhat important	26	33	6	28	14
Not too important	26	27	23	15	11
Not at all important	27	12	69	20	19
No answer	1	1	<1	2	7
	100	100	100	100	100
Belief in God					
Believe in God of Bible	26	33	7	46	64
Believe in other higher power/spiritual force	50	51	48	44	25
Don't believe in either	22	14	44	8	6
Unclear	2	3	1	1	5
	100	100	100	100	100

Note: Figures may not add to 100% due to rounding.
Source: Survey conducted Nov. 19, 2019-June 3, 2020, among U.S. adults.
"Jewish Americans in 2020"

PEW RESEARCH CENTER

All that said, there is reason to be optimistic. Jews have survived so many calamities in their history that, as Mark Twain once announced: "Reports of my death have been greatly exaggerated." Israeli founding father David Ben Gurion had an even better quote, regarding Israel's success in wars against its much larger neighbors: "Anyone who doesn't believe in miracles isn't a realist." The Fall of 2023 marks the beginning of the 5,784th year of the Jewish calendar. A long list of seemingly invincible empires has risen and fallen during that time, but Jews keep the faith and find a way to persevere.

And so it is with First Congregation Sons of Israel. Its history, traditions, and beautiful building give it enormous appeal, with the potential to grow and prosper not hard to imagine, as St. Johns County around it has grown and prospered over the last number of years. With the lights still on in 5784, it maintains its status as not only the oldest synagogue in St. Augustine, but the oldest continuously used synagogue in all of Florida. Which is not to say that FCSI hasn't kept up with the times. If you've read this far, go ahead and check out the synagogue's website: https://www.firstcongregationsonsofisrael.com/ and also its Facebook page: https://www.facebook.com/historicsynagogue .

ACKNOWLEDGMENTS

Many thanks to the knowledgeable synagogue officers and elder statesmen and women who sat down with me, or spoke with me on the phone for oral interviews. Key among these were FCSI President Les Stern, Simone Broudy-Kilbourn, Suzanne Lichter, Rene Naughton, Dulcy Freeman, Reggie Daniels, and Rabbis Mona Decker and Joel Fox. Charles Tingley, the Senior Research Librarian at the St. Augustine Historical Society not only directed me to the library's own resources, but also suggested other leads that I followed to collect more information. He himself wrote a paper on the synagogue in Atlanta where the FCSI stained-glass windows were originally installed. As if all that weren't enough, Mr. Tingley scrubbed the manuscript and found a few historical errors, which I fixed. Karen Stern has been instrumental in connecting me with contacts in the community, and promoting the history-book project among the membership. And finally, a big shout-out to my very talented niece, graphic artist Diana Blau, who designed the bookcover.

NOTES

Foreward

[1] Photo by Byron Capo, taken at annual membership meeting.

[2] https://tourpass.com/st-augustine/st-augustine-first-time-visitor-guide/

Chapter 2 - Origins

[3] For more information, this is their website: https://sajhs.com/

[4] "Casa Shalom Journal," Spring 2000; Volume 3, Issue 1, pp. 6-7.

[5] "Florida Jewish Heritage Trail, 2000, Florida Department of State, Division of Historical Resources, pp 10, 15; Also found in www.jewishvirtuallibrary.org/david-yulee-levy.

[6] https://www.jewishvirtuallibrary.org/the-pale-of-settlement.

[7] The Torah, or the Five Books of Moses, are the first five books of the bible: Genesis, Exodus, Leviticus, Numbers, and Deuteronomy. Don't even consider appearing on Jeopardy! without knowing this.

[8] From www.visitstaugustine.com

[9] St. Augustine Evening Record, September 15, 2009.

[10] Giordano, Stephanie, "A Small Story of a Commercial Building in St. Augustine," (2022) Touring Lincolnville: A Celebration of Historic Black Business.

[11] Photos reprinted with permission from First Congregation Sons of Israel collection.

[12] Minnie's photo from www.genicom; Groucho's from https://it.wikipedia.org/wiki/File:Groucho_Marx.jpg

[13] Transcript, Mary Safer, Oral History Interview with Samuel Proctor, November 28, 1989, pp 2-14, Samuel Proctor Oral History Program Collection, P.K. Yonge Library of Florida History, University of Florida.

[14] From the St. Augustine Historical Society Reference Library synagogue collection.

Chapter 3 - Cemetery

[15] St. Augustine Record, March 8, 1911.

[16] Photo via "Street View" in Google Maps.

[17] From the St. Augustine Historical Society Reference Library synagogue collection.

[18] St. Augustine Record, February 18, 2019.

[19] From Simone Broudy-Kilbourn's private collection.

Chapter 4 - Building

[20] Information in this section sourced to articles in the St. Augustine Evening Record on the dates following the events described.

[21] The letters B and V in Spanish are virtually interchangeable.

[22] From www.scip.be.

[23] From First Congregation Sons of Israel Facebook page.

[24] Ibid.

[25] From First Congregation Sons of Israel's collection.

[26] Over 850,000 Jews from Arab countries were either expelled or fled in the wake of the establishment of Israel in 1948. Great Jewish communities, such as in Aleppo, Syria, simply ceased to exist. These 1948 refugees formed the basis of Israel's Sephardic population. Arab refugees from 1948 (identified as Palestinians since the 1960s), originally of a smaller number, are the ones that have attracted considerable media attention and United Nations' funding.

[27] I would recommend reading Leo Rosten's *The Joys of Yiddish*, a glossary of the language, including situational context, and of course, jokes.

[28] The author was an English and Social Studies teacher at Torah Academy from 2014-2016.

[29] From First Congregation Sons of Israel's collection.

[30] From St. Augustine Historical Society Research Library, Synagogue collection.

Chapter 5 – Stained Glass

[31] Transcript, Mary Safer, Oral History Interview...pp.32-33.

[32] St. Augustine Evening Record, October 27, 1924.

[33] Interview with Les Stern, July 20, 2023.

[34] Photo by the author.

[35] Photo by the author.

Chapter 6 – Through the Years

[36] 2023 Goldring/Woldenberg Institute of Southern Jewish Life.

[37] Ibid, citing State Archives of Florida.

[38] Op. Cit., October 5, 2015. Much of the information also appeared in a St. Augustine Record article entitled "It Happened Here," published in a weekend edition, August 9-10, 1975, p. 9.

[39] From Simone Broudy-Kilbourn's private collection.

[40] From the St. Augustine Historical Society Research Library Synagogue collection.

[41] https://www.floridashistoriccoast.com/things-to-do/history/historic-architecture/.

[42] St Augustine Record clipping from St. Augustine Historical Society Research Library synagogue collection.

[43] St. Augustine Record, October20, 1990.

[44] St. Augustine Record, March 12, 1999.

[45] Photo by author. Decorative curtains were a gift from the Naughton family.

[46] St Augustine Record clipping from the St. Augustine Historical Society Research library synagogue collection.

[47] St. Augustine Record, February 11, 2010.

Chapter 7 - Leaders

[48] Craig's Funeral Home Online Obituary Historic City News (online) November 5, 2021.

[49] Historic City News (online), November 5, 2021.

[50] St. Augustine Record, January 24, 2004.

[51] Craig Funeral Home Obituary: https://www.craigfuneralhome.com/obituaries/MaxDavid-Jaffe-36006/#/PhotosVideos.

[52] St. Augustine Record, September 22, 1987.

[53] February 1951 photo provided by Suzanne Lichter.

[54] A Bris is performed by a Mohel (rhymes with boil) on the 8th day of a baby's life, and is based on the original such circumcision, which sealed a covenant (which is what "Bris" means in Hebrew) between Abraham and G_d.

[55] Photo (at right) by author.

[56] From Suzanne Lichter's private collection.

[57] Ibid. Photo of display case taken by author.

[58] Op. Cit., pp.45-48.

[59] From https://www.legacy.com/us/obituaries/staugustine/name/philip-bernstein-obituary?id=7588617.

[60] St. Augustine Record, May 1 2013.

[61] St. Augustine Record, September 18, 1998.

[62] From Simone Broudy-Kilbourn's private collection.

[63] Ibid.

[64] Ibid.

[65] Ibid.

[66] From Karen Stern's Facebook page.

[67] Interview with Rene Naughton at her home, August 14, 2023.

[68] From Rene Naughton's private collection.

[69] Photo by the author.

Chapter 8 – Storm Damage

[70] Photo by Byron Capo.

[71] From the Hurricane Matthew Wikipedia entry: https://en.wikipedia.org/wiki/Hurricane_Matthew.

[72] Photo from FCSI Facebook page.

[73] St. Augustine Record, May 18, 2018.

[74] Op. Cit., August 24, 2018.

Chapter 9 - Security

[75] From www.fortmose.org.

[76] From Saint Aug. Jewish Historical Society Website: https://sajhs.com/history/

[77] Rene Naughton remembers a swastika incident in the late 1970s. It is not clear if this was the same one as referred to by Les Stern with differing recollections as to the date, or if there were two such incidents.

Chapter 10 – The Synagogue Today

[78] Photo from FCSI Facebook page.

[79] "Aliyah" is also the term used for the process through which a Diaspora Jew immigrates to Israel.

[80] An annual Jewish harvest festival, which falls within a week after Yom Kippur.

[81] Phone interview with the author, August 18, 2023.

[82] Photo from online bio page.

Chapter 11 - Conclusion

[83] https://www.jewishvirtuallibrary.org/jewish-population-in-the-united-states-nationally.

[84] Sources are indicated at the bottom of the graphic image.

About the Author

Born and raised in the New York area, Robert Blau studied undergrad at Brandeis University, did a two-year stint in the Peace Corps in West Africa, then went to grad school at Ohio University. Soon after obtaining a Master's degree in International Affairs, he joined the U.S. Department of State as a Foreign Service Officer, serving for over 30 years until his retirement in 2014. Overseas tours included Santo Domingo, Conakry (Guinea), Brasilia, Panama, Lisbon, Havana and San Salvador, where he was Chargé d'Affaires for twenty months. He had domestic assignments at the State Department in Washington DC dealing with Bosnia reconstruction, International Narcotics and Crime, Cuban Affairs, and Human Resources. He also was assigned for two years as a faculty member of the Air War College at Maxwell Air Force Base.

After retirement he worked as a teacher at Torah Academy of Jacksonville, dabbled in resume writing, and then returned to Washington to be Vice President for Operations at the Millennium Challenge Corporation.

He returned to Florida in 2018, moving to Saint Augustine, and joining First Congregation Sons of Israel, where his father, of blessed memory, had been a congregant. Fully absorbed in the Oldest City's history, Robert has served as a volunteer at Castillo San Marcos, dressing up as a 1740 Spanish soldier and greeting the visitors. He published a short e-book in the summer of 2023 about his experiences battling throat and neck cancer entitled "Cancer World."

www.ingramcontent.com/pod-product-compliance
Lightning Source LLC
Chambersburg PA
CBHW070537160726
48003CB00004B/1806

9798223735717